Praise for **Serious Fun**...

"This book will wake up, inspire and most important, raise the bar for those we entrust with our meetings."

— **Seth Godin**, best-selling author, *Your Turn*

"If you're new to adventure programming, buy this book; it's all you need to get started in the right direction, and keep you there."

— **Karl Rohnke**, best-selling author, *Silver Bullets*

"We've all been to workshops & events that are just plain dull & boring. Now, there's really no excuse. Mark generously shares a ton of practical advice and free resources to help you make your events more engaging. I love his quote – 'Let's take fun more seriously' – this sums up the book perfectly. Great for speakers, educators, trainers – anyone ready to lead the revolution against dull, boring & ineffective events."

— **Andrew Griffiths**, Australia's #1 small business & entrepreneurial author

"Serious Fun captures how Mark engages people. He is a master of delivering fantastic programs and this book brings it all together so that we can all learn how to run great programs too!"

— **Wendy Lewis**, CEO Girl Guides Victoria

"Mark absolutely nails it. He is, truly, a programming ninja."

— **Ryan Eller**, founder Paradigm Shift, co-host *'Live Your List'* podcast

"Mark's expertise & depth of knowledge in facilitating adventure has been highly valued by all of our students for many years & has led to some real breakthroughs in learning & understanding. Now, to have those many years of experience & expertise within this book, is priceless."

– **Andrew Davis**, Co-ordinator Outdoor Recreation Leadership, Wodonga TAFE

"This book is about genuinely connecting with people, your tribe, in the most fun & engaging way – a must-have component in a successful program."

– **Anoushka Gungadin**, CEO The Duke of Edinburgh Awards Australia, Victoria

"This book is 'seriously fun!' There were countless ideas that had me jumping up to write things down in a notebook, and at least 10 concrete, actionable ideas that I put into practice the following day with a program I was leading! Fantastic!"

– **Chad Littlefield**, adventure educator, creator *'We! Connect'* Cards

"Every camp leader should read this book before their campers arrive. Mark knows what he's talking about, and has tons of practical experience to back it up. A sure-fire method to engage young people, develop their cooperation skills and have fun."

– **Lauren Popkin Herschthal**, Owner / Director, Blue Star Camps, USA

"Serious Fun is full of creative ideas that can be used by trainers and facilitators to develop their full range of skills. Even if you find that you've stumbled into a few of these ideas on your own, this book dives deeper into why all educators should take fun more seriously."

– **Richard Ross**, CEO, Project Adventure Inc

"As valuable as Mark's other books and website (playmeo!) may be for providing activity ideas to trainers, this book is incredibly more important – Serious Fun offers the step-by-step how-to's that ensure those activities are successfully facilitated. This book gives you the methodology of a four part process that will help you to make your next event more relevant and enjoyable."

– **Sean Glaze**, corporate team-building facilitator & speaker

serious
FUN

Your Step-by-Step Guide
To Leading Remarkably Fun Programs
That Make A Difference

MARK COLLARD

www.seriousfunbook.com
www.playmeo.com

let's take fun more seriously ...

Hey Catherine!
Have FUNN

Published by Mark Collard
PO Box 4237, Croydon Hills VIC 3136
hello@playmeo.com

ABN 64 829 426 721

National Library of Australia Cataloging-in-Publication entry

Collard, Mark, 1964-
Serious Fun: Your Step-by-Step Guide To Leading Remarkably Fun Programs That Make A Difference / Mark Collard
First edition 2014, Reprint 2015

ISBN 978-0-9925464-0-3 (paperback)

Activity programs in education
Active learning
Educational change
Educational psychology
Employees – Training of
Teams in the workplace – Training of
Group work in education
Group games

Dewey Number 371.3

Cover design by BespokeBookCovers
Internal layout design by Squeezebox
Photos by Morrison Photography

Printed in Australia by Griffin Press
Printed in USA by Edwards Brothers Malloy

To Gilly
who blesses my life with her infinite love,

and Devon
whose smile reflects the essence of serious fun,
every day.

Contents

If You Haven't Got
A Lot Of Time

Key Messages

This book describes a simple, four-step sequence I use to create remarkably fun programs.

If you want to lead programs that are fun and make a difference to the lives and performance of your group, then I'm talking to you. Specifically, teachers, corporate trainers, youth leaders, camp leaders, outdoor educators, etc.

Many program leaders adopt an out-dated, boring approach to program design and delivery, which leads to unmotivated participants, unproductive teams and unrewarding outcomes. It doesn't have to be this way.

Group leaders commonly make one (or more) of seven mistakes when leading their programs:

1. Not Breaking the Ice

2. Lack of Philosophical Framework

3. Unrealistic Expectations

4. Poor Needs Analysis

5. Not Valuing People's Time

6. Neglecting the Power of Story

7. Absence of Fun

Environment dictates performance. The key to leading programs which are outrageously fun and make a difference to the groups you work with is the type of environment you create.

I have developed a powerful sequence that you can use to intentionally create this environment, every time. This approach is not about being different, it is focused on creating a difference.

Having fun is the key. Honouring choice, valuing people and providing opportunities for growth and interaction with others are also critically important.

Key Methodology

This is the four-step sequence I call the *Difference Model*:

Step 1 – Needs Analysis (Plan)

This step asks, what difference is your program going to make (to your group)? This task is more than just setting goals, it's about clearly identifying how you want your group to be feeling at the end of your program.

Applies to: any space in which groups gather.

Step 2 – Setting The Tone (Prime)

Your leadership role: Coach

This step intentionally creates a fun, safe and supportive environment, where choice is honoured and trust is built. All interaction occurs within your group's Comfort Zone, i.e., that space within which people feel inspired and comfortable to interact with one another.

Applies to: conference openings, start-of-year orientations, new project teams.

Step 3 – Doing The Work (Pump)

Your leadership role: Facilitator

Operating within a clearly defined framework which values people and provides opportunities for growth, this step invites your group to develop it's communication, problem-solving and responsibility skills. Much of this interaction occurs within your group's Stretch Zone, i.e., that space which invites your group to build on its strengths and abilities to function more effectively.

Applies to: team-building programs, youth meetings, adventure programs, school classrooms.

Step 4 – The Difference (Peak)

Your leadership role: Partner

Following this sequence, using the tools available to you, and doing everything you can to prepare your group will give them the best chance of not only getting what they came for, but so much more. The most rewarding outcome of this unique approach is experienced in the way your program leaves people feeling – engaged, empowered, valued and meaningfully connected to others.

Applies to: any group that wants to have fun while making a difference.

having fun is the key ...

Preface

A man was walking across the desert, stumbling, almost dying of thirst, when he saw a well. As he approached the well, he found a note in a can close by. The note read:

"Dear friend, there is enough water in this well, enough for all, but sometimes the leather washer gets dried up and you have to prime the pump. Now, if you look underneath the rock just west of the well, you will find a bottle full of water, corked. Please don't drink the water. What you've got to do is take the bottle of water and pour the first half very slowly into the well to loosen up the leather washer. Then pour the rest in very quickly and pump like crazy! You will get water. The well has never run dry. Have faith. And when you're done, don't forget to put the note back, fill up the bottle and put it back under the rock. Good luck. Have a fun trip. Sincerely, your friend Desert Pete."

– Tim Hansel, author *Holy Sweat*

What would you do?

You're desperate for water, about to expire from dehydration, and yet, in reality, the bottle of water is only enough to quench your thirst, not save your life. Would you risk it all?

This story is a powerful allegory about some of the essential elements of this book. As I see it, you have three choices.

First, you could read the note, choose to drink all of the water and move on in your journey.

Second, you could drink a little of the water, and attempt to use the remainder to prime the pump.

Or, third, you could follow the instructions.

The first choice is akin to reading this book, nodding your head and continuing on your way. And this is fine. It is, of course, a choice. However, choosing not to add value (to your program, your skills, a significant relationship, etc) is the same as taking it away. Your thirst for knowledge may be quenched, but you may have missed an opportunity to benefit many of the groups you work with today and tomorrow, not to mention, the leaders of these groups who follow you.

This first choice reminds me of the long-term consequences of the cat which jumps onto a hot stove top. The cat will never jump onto a hot stove again, and that is good, but it will never jump onto the stove when it is cold either. Such is the experience of many people who have endured a boring, embarrassing or down-right threatening group experience in the past. They will baulk at the prospect of repeating this experience a second or third, or tenth time, no matter how 'safe' it may, in fact, be.

The second choice is a bit like hedging your bets, akin to placing a foot on both sides of a barbed-wire fence – a move in any direction is likely to cause harm. Having drunk some of the water, you are likely to thirst again very soon, but worse, you will give up pumping because, no matter how hard you work, you won't have enough of the vital ingredients to allow the pump to function properly. On paper, your program may promise to strike water, but in practice, it may fail to live up to its full potential, because – no matter how well intentioned you may be – its capacity to make a difference will be stunted by a poor design.

The third choice, my invitation to you, dear reader, will take courage. It's a risk. There is plenty of evidence in this book that will point you to a powerful way to draw water from your programming well. Yet, can you trust me? You may hear me asking you to pour the only water you are sure of (your experience, your qualifications, your intuition, etc) down the well. That is certainly not true – you do not need to turn your back on all that you know. But, understand this – in learning, there is risk.

I expect, also, to challenge some of your long-held, pre-conceived notions about how to break the ice, encourage people to participate, build trust, strengthen relationships, etc. I'm not saying that you don't know what you're doing, but I will invite you to stretch beyond what you already know. And consider that, with the right sort of preparation, there is always more value (water) to pump out of your program.

Finally, there is the instruction to work. This book is not a lazy person's guide to program design. Do not mistake the simple four-step methodology I shall describe to you as a substitute for work. I, along with Desert Pete remind you, that after you trust and risk, you must pump like crazy if you want to make a difference.

My only promise is that once you know how to drill for water, you will never want to sip from a small bottle again.

you must pump like crazy if you want to make a difference ...

part one
PLAN

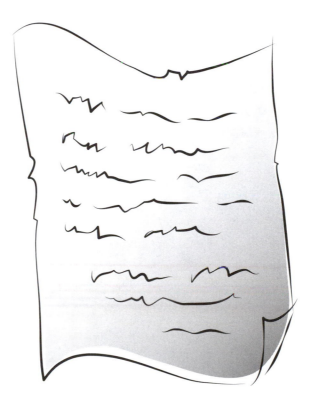

The Note

"You never climb a mountain on accident
– it has to be intentional."

– Mark Udall, US congressman

I have applied the same approach to the writing of this book, as the methodology I share within it.

Accordingly, Part One is my plan, in which I create a map of the territory, and survey the path to freedom. You will learn who I'm talking to, why I'm talking to you, and how I plan to talk to you.

In Part Two, I equip you with all of the necessary thinking to prepare you for your journey. Without risk, you will learn the mistakes you should avoid, the best way to travel, and the benefits of trying something new.

In Part Three, we do the work that matters. Step by step, you will learn everything you need to know, along with the tools you need to carry, to create remarkably fun programs which make a difference to your group. It is simple, but not always easy.

Finally, in Part Four, we take what you have learned and apply it in practice – again and again, in many different situations.

1

Are You Talking To Me?

If you run programs, events or any sort of gathering which involves groups of people – students, staff, strangers, volunteers, young and old – then the answer is an emphatic YES.

If you design and deliver programs for the purpose of recreation, education, professional or personal development, then YES, I am talking to you, too.

Two-minute programs. Year-long programs. Five people. Five thousand people. YES.

But, most critical of all, if you want to lead programs and do 'work' that matters – that which is fun and makes a difference to your group – then I'm talking to you.

The approach, strategies and leadership tips I share in this book apply to pretty much every group-based program, event or gathering you could care to name. So, if you're a...

- classroom teacher
- corporate trainer
- outdoor educator
- adventure / experiential educator
- conference and event organiser

- Scout or Girl Guide leader
- camp leader
- youth leader
- group therapist
- sports team coach

... or one of many other positions of leadership, I am talking to you.

Just so you know...

... this book has been written by an Australian. My nationality is irrelevant, except to say, that from birth, I have learned to speak in metric, and I am compelled to add the letter 'u' to many words such as colour, labour and favourite, or substitute the letter 'z' for 's' on occasions.

No matter where you are from, I am glad that you are here. Feel free to convert and overlook the different letters at will.

2

What Difference Do You Want To Make?

"Act as if what you do makes a difference. It does."
– William James, philosopher

A classroom of students look up at their teacher with empty eyes, bored out of their brains thinking 'same old, same old.'

An auditorium is filled with seasoned conference delegates keeping to themselves, concerned that someone may sit next to them.

With eyes focused anywhere other than the front of the room, you ask for someone to stand up and introduce themselves, to kick off your training session.

Do these situations sound familiar to you? Maybe you see yourself in them? Do you wish there was an alternative? There is, and this book reveals the answer.

Every one of these situations is a sad reflection of a poor and out-dated approach to programming.

Imagine, instead, a class filled with students, all leaning in and eagerly participating in your discussion. Or a conference room filled with warmth and laughter long before the keynote speaker has entered the room. Or, consider for a moment, your dilemma if every hand shot up when you needed a willing volunteer.

If you are responsible for the design and delivery of some form of group-based program – a school classroom, staff training course, conference, youth group evening, residential camp, etc – then I expect you want the most powerful and rewarding outcome possible for your group. This book will show you how, in four clearly defined steps, answering many of your questions along the way.

I've delivered countless programs for hundreds of groups and organisations all over the world, and I know that the most satisfying and successful programs – for the participants and the leader – are those which intentionally promote interaction, build trust and take fun seriously right from the start.

Notice, I said 'intentionally' and 'right from the start.' You see, good outcomes don't just happen. They are created, in the same way water is drawn from Desert Pete's well. There are certain elements which have to be present – instructions, strategy, risk, effort – to produce the desired results. Without these elements, all you have is potential, and potential on its own is not enough to satisfy your thirst.

To this end, simply throwing a bunch of people together, even with a purpose, does not make a group work. When this occurs – and it does, a lot – this is what I've noticed...

If there's no trust, people pull back from participating fully. If there's no fun, people find it difficult to engage – with the content or with others. And if there's no challenge, there's only boredom and no opportunity for growth. The result? Unhappy people, unsatisfactory results and unfulfilled expectations. Un, un, un.

For more than 25 years, program leaders have come to me because they experience three common problems. In essence, they want to remove the 'un:'

- They find it difficult to engage unmotivated or unwilling participants;
- They lead groups which don't often get along, or are unproductive; and
- They are given too little time to produce unrealistic outcomes.

If one or more of these issues strikes a chord with you, then you're in the right place.

This book will share a unique methodology which acknowledges the fact that, by our very nature, people don't like to step outside their comfort zones. As complex beings, humans have continued to exist as a species because of a primal instinct to survive. Consequently, if a program is not fun, or people feel threatened or there's any chance that they will look foolish, the program will fail to achieve its full potential. And yet, some program leaders wonder why they meet resistance.

In the chapters which follow, I describe a simple, yet powerful four-step model, which I call the *Difference Model*. It will equip you with the skills and strategies you need to prepare your group for success right from the start, ultimately helping you to deliver an extremely powerful program which you and your group will thoroughly enjoy.

This unique approach appeals to people of all ages, and works with nearly every type of program and curricula you can think of.

At a glance, this is what you can look forward to:

1. Needs Analysis (Plan)

Just as the man in our desert story would have died of thirst if he did not uncover the note (no plan at all), he most certainly would have been unable to do more than quench his thirst if he had neglected to follow the instructions (the plan) and drank the water in the small bottle.

This, the first deliberate step, is as critical as that desert note. You need a plan to guide your actions.

In much the same way an annual budget means little more than an expression of an organisation's priorities, this step is the starting point for the preparation and work which must follow. Things change, but without a clearly defined target, you may as well pack up and go home.

You will learn how to set a target. This section will also help you to explore the questions you need to ask to fully understand your group and the task ahead of you, and – importantly – the difference you intend to make in your program or event. You can expect all of the regular questions to form an important part of your 'needs analysis,' and a couple, too, I suspect, which will challenge your thinking.

Then, with note in hand, you are ready to get busy.

2. Setting the Tone (Prime)

Get this step right – it's not hard, but it is critical – and everything which follows will be so much easier and significantly more successful. It's the step most program leaders under-estimate.

This step sets the tone and begins the sensitive process of preparing your group and switching on their brains. Ask for too much – by not adding the right amount of water to loosen the washer – and you'll frighten your group away. But, progress too slowly – neglect to pump when you should – and there's a potential for boredom.

There are several key elements involved in this step which will help you 'break the ice' and, critically, create a platform upon which your group (and program) will thrive. But, note, this step is not about playing ice breaker games. It's about breaking the ice, and, yes, there is a difference. If you or your group cringe at the thought of 'ice-breakers,' then study this step carefully because I'll reveal five reasons why most 'ice-breakers' don't work.

For programs which gather people for only a short period of time – conferences for example – these first two steps may be all you need to apply. Whereas, for longer term programs, once your group is switched on, they will be ready to follow your lead onto the next challenge or whatever your program demands.

3. Doing the Work (Pump)

If you jump to this stage too early (which many program leaders do), you can expect trouble. Trouble looks like unwillingness to participate, put-downs, excuses, asking for too much in too little time, a lack of responsibility, just to name a few of the usual suspects.

All of these issues can be avoided – or at a minimum, mitigated – by adhering to the key elements of the Prime stage, which will prepare your group to willingly step outside their 'Comfort zone' into what is commonly referred to as their 'Stretch zone.'

This step will develop your group's hidden potential, to flex and build their muscles (so to speak) for bigger and better things. It's not rocket science, but this step subscribes to the common understanding that the more you train and flex your muscles, the stronger you can expect to become.

As this process can take time, and you may need to pump like crazy on occasions, you may ask, "Why bother?" Two simple reasons:

- If you really want to set your group up for the most powerful and rewarding experience possible (that's why you're here, isn't it?), why would you give your group only half a glass of water, when they are sitting on a well?
- This step intentionally builds trust and strengthens relationships, the bedrock of group success, no matter the difference you're trying to make in your program.

Do the work, pump like crazy, and you can expect more fun, more participation, more value – in this order.

4. The Difference (Peak)

Appropriately primed and pumped up, this final stage is the holy grail of programming – the ticking of boxes, the getting of stuff done, the reaching for stars.

Now is the best time to deliver your content, develop those skills and extract the highest quality water from your group's well – it's the reason your group has gathered, and is the reason your program exists. Learning to swim, networking with strangers, constructing a complex sentence, solving interesting problems, delivering a keynote presentation, developing team skills, and so on.

From a classroom filled with students to a corporate training room, or a conference auditorium filled with unfamiliar faces to a weekly youth group meeting. The more effort and time you invest in the development of your group (pumping like crazy), especially early on, the more powerful and rewarding your program (or event or gathering) will be.

So, what difference do you want to make?

The Most Frequently Asked Question

I deliver training workshops all over the world, and by far the most common question I get is this – "How do you do what you do?" or in other words, "What steps do I take to achieve the results I get?"

This book is my response.

It is the first definitive step-by-step guide designed specifically to help novice and experienced program leaders create remarkably fun programs which produce the most powerful and rewarding outcomes possible. Why? To help you make a difference in the world.

The strategies and leadership tips I share can be applied to almost ANY group-based program, from a two-minute conference energiser to a dynamic semester-long curriculum. It's light on theory, easy to use, and can be applied quickly by ordinary people with little or no cost.

Then, underpinned by my four-step programming model, I explore dozens of practical solutions to answer many more frequently-asked questions, such as:

- Where do I start?
- How do I get everyone to participate?
- How do I break the ice?
- What can I do to help my team function better?
- How do I manage difficult behaviours, such as a dominant personality?
- What are the best ways to divide large groups into smaller groups?
- How can I draw more value from my group's experience?
- How can I manage large groups on my own?
- How can I achieve unrealistic outcomes with too little time?
- What do I do to make my job easier?

I share the best of my knowledge drawn from 25+ years of trial and error programming with tens of thousands of people from all over the world. I believe this wisdom, and that borrowed from my peers, will scaffold your program for unbelievable success and leave your group feeling incredibly engaged, valued and inspired, exceeding all of their (and your) expectations.

If you want to have fun, do work that matters and make a difference, then I invite you to embrace the approach I share in this book.

I hope you do. Your group will thank you for it.

the more effort and time you invest in the development of your group, the more powerful and rewarding your program will be ...

part two
PRIME

The Bottle of Water

"Always do your best.
What you plant now you will harvest later."

– Og Mandino, author

There are a few things that I'd like to share with you before we charge head-long into the four steps of my programming model.

By all means, skip ahead and start absorbing the details of my methodology. You'll find what you need to get started.

However, gaining first an understanding of the philosophical framework of my approach, not to mention the research which underpins it, will help you to make sense of my programming model and the practical solutions at the back of the book.

I expect also that the next few sections will answer some key questions you may have at this point, such as:

- Who am I, and why should you listen to me?
- What sort of problems will this book solve?
- Is the approach I share scientifically researched and proven?
- What's in it for you?

In other words, this Part will prime you, set the tone, for the rest of the book.

3

In Your Shoes

I've been in your shoes. Well, not your actual shoes, but you know what I mean.

My name is Mark and I'm a professional training consultant. I'm the author of two top-selling publications in the training and education field, and with more than 25 years of experience working with thousands of people all over the world, I know what it's like to work with groups that...

... worry they're going to be asked to do something embarrassing;

... don't want to move from their seats;

... are not interested or are unwilling to participate;

... don't get along, or don't work well together;

... are made up of people who have been forced to attend;

... exhibit anti-social and / or difficult behaviours;

... waste a lot time waiting for people to arrive;

... are so large that it's very easy for some people to hide;

... ask for too much in too little time;

... and ...

... I'm sure you could add many, many more 'types' to this list.

These groups have been the bread and butter of my career. Of course, I have worked with many more wonderfully co-operative, playful and talented groups too, but the truth is – I cut my programming teeth on the rough edges of these less-than-ideal, but wholly worthy groups.

Oh, the fun I have had inviting each and every one of these groups to play, share and interact. Yet, as I have juggled all of these issues, I have often wondered if others felt the same way I do...

On occasion, I'd come home at the end of a difficult program, and start to doubt my ability to cut through the crap and make a difference.

I'd sometimes look out at the sea of faces before me and wonder if they're going to like me. Deep down, I really just want to know that I'm good enough and worthy of their love.

I've slumped in my bed at the end of a day, exhausted from 'putting out fires' and generating all of the energy in my program, and wake in the morning to find the bedroom light still on.

I've waded through dozens of activity books which promise tons of fun and interaction, but not one of them tells me how to apply these experiences to my group.

Then, on the flip-side as a participant, I have looked at others in my group to see the same look of discomfort in their eyes as yet another inappropriate group activity is introduced.

Tell me, did you see yourself in any of these situations?

All of them (and many, many more) have caused me to wonder if there was a better way.

There is.

In My Shoes

I'm on a mission to transform the design and delivery of group-based programs, from so-so to awesome.

I want to transform your experience of the time you spend in front of groups from that of "Oh no, here we go again," to "Wow, that was amazing!"

I've been in your shoes. There is a better way. It's time we changed our thinking and our approach.

That's what this book is all about.

4

Seven Mistakes Program Leaders Make

"People will forget what you said.
People will forget what you did.
But, people will never forget how you made them feel."

– Maya Angelou, author

To be fair, most of the problems I described on the page you just turned are not actually problems – they are symptoms. They are what shows up, or manifests, when one or more problems lurk in the background.

For example, people not willing to participate in your program could, perhaps, be a symptom of an 'unsafe' or unfriendly atmosphere. Late arrivals could be a symptom of, perhaps, not giving your group a reason to arrive on time. And so on.

I fervently believe that approach is everything. That is, everything that you do and don't do during the life of your program – before, during and after – will impact your group and therefore, your program outcomes.

Your program does not start once you have everyone's attention, or resume when your group returns from the lunch break. Who you are being, and the approach you adopt – which significantly influences the way people are feeling and interacting – will determine your program's success.

If you drill down deep enough into the most common issues, you will uncover a handful of mistakes, and they all come under the heading of 'approach.'

Yes, yes, I know, there are groups out there which even their own mothers find difficult to love (I've worked with them too), suggesting that no matter how good your program is, these folks will always give you trouble. Yeah, I get that. But, the truth is you can't change how people think or what they do without, first, changing how they feel. To this end, you are well advised to focus all of your efforts on your approach because it is one of the most powerful tools (to influence how people feel) at your disposal.

... you can't change how people think or what they do without, first, changing how they feel

That said, here are the top seven mistakes I believe program leaders make that get them into all sorts of trouble...

1. Not Breaking the Ice
or Asking Too Much Too Soon

By far the most serious, far-reaching mistake program leaders make is not adequately breaking the ice, that is, failing to remove the obstacles which prevent people from fully and safely interacting with others and the program.

Fundamentally, this is the source of almost all of the issues described so far, and possibly those which persist in your group right now. Indeed, I'll even be so bold as to say – if you're meeting resistance anywhere in your program, then I'll 'wager a tenner' that you have not adequately thawed the 'ice' that your group is experiencing.

I fervently believe that if people are not having fun, or do not feel valued or there's any chance that they could look foolish in front of others, they will find it very difficult to willingly and fully engage in your program, no matter the purpose of the group experience – whether they're at school, at work, in training or at play.

Basically, any task that requires an individual or a group of people to step outside of their 'Comfort zones' (more on this later) before they are ready to do so, will trigger a set of feelings, behaviours and survival instincts which may ultimately stunt the success of your program. Or, to put it simply, asking too much too soon puts people off.

Ice forms when strangers, meeting for the first time, are asked to share their most embarrassing moments. Or, it will develop immediately the prospect of having to speak in front of others presents itself. Ice will also form when something or someone challenges a group's long-held beliefs.

Arriving late, making excuses, deliberately sitting two seats away from one another, lying, acting out, and looking down at the ground are all great examples of ice manifesting itself. The more ice you have, the more difficult it will be to achieve your program goals.

A more powerful approach is to always expect it to be present – even among people who know each other very well. There is always ice, even if only to your program, so prepare accordingly.

Later, I will share a simple check list which you can easily apply to your program to help you break the ice effectively. Do this well, and you will not only attract significantly more participation, but the quality of the interaction will open up many new opportunities for your group.

2. Lack of Philosophical Framework
or Environment Dictates Performance

In my experience, most programs lack a powerful philosophical grounding because this is what I see and hear people say all the time:

"They said we had a choice, but we rarely got to exercise it."

"I often feel under pressure not to say anything."

"There's not many of us, but I feel invisible."

"We had a lot of fun, but I have no idea what this has to do with ...."

If these comments sound familiar to you, this may be a sign that your programmatic philosophy is out of whack. It's more than just the impact of mixed messages – it's the difference between an approach that supports your program goals, or one that runs counter to it.

Your philosophical framework is the lens through which you view the world, your program and the people in it. For example, if you view people as, or expect them to be, obedient, you will rarely give them a choice. If you believe that learning is self-evident, then you won't bother to extract meaning from an experience. If you think people tend to feel and act like you do, then you'll expect them to speak up for themselves, or take the initiative, or willingly try something new for the first time, and so on.

I don't know about your experience, but these beliefs do not match the psychology of the thousands of people I have worked with over the years.

Generally speaking, when people feel threatened, or disempowered, or have no idea what they are doing (all of which stem from an unhealthy environment) they tend to pull back from participating fully, or worse, actively sabotage you, the group or the program.

The truth is that environment dictates performance. The more powerful the environment, the more powerful you can expect your results to be. No matter if your group has just met for the first time, or they have been together for many years – anything you can do which will positively influence the environment within which your group may interact will help you to produce more satisfying results every time.

In Part Three, I will share five useful tools that you can use to help you avoid this mistake, and develop the hallmarks of a powerful philosophical framework.

3. Unrealistic Expectations
or Assuming You Already Know

The first two 'mistakes' are the most common, and arguably, the most debilitating features of a poor programming approach. Having unrealistic expectations pops up as another big problem.

We all know the importance of setting goals. As the saying goes, how can you possibly know if you've arrived if you don't know where you're going. This is true, but as important as this process is, I'm not referring just to the process of setting clearly defined goals.

The mistake I refer to, of forming unrealistic expectations, focuses on three key issues.

First, while solving a group's needs or problems is very important, the more important task is problem-finding. While it is clearly very important to solve the problem, as distinguished from the symptom, it is critical that you focus on the right problem. For example, I know of some groups which have been sent away on expensive team-building exercises, when the real problem remained behind sitting in the manager's office. In these cases, the expressed need for 'team building' was really a misnomer for the manager just wanting his or her staff to "do what they're told to do."

Second, sometimes what the client or group is expecting is altogether different from what the program leader is prepared to deliver. Mostly, this is caused by poor communication, but it is just as damaging to the program, as much as it is to the group's success. A striking example comes to mind...

A father and son group I led many years ago arrived one weekend fully expecting to climb the high ropes course at the end of the day. Fair enough, too, because this was the clearly defined and communicated goal of our program. However, within minutes of getting off the bus, it was apparent that this group did not share a high regard for safety or procedures. Later in the day, as the behaviour of the group deteriorated, I had to decide if I would permit the group to harness-up and climb the high elements. On the basis that this group had not demonstrated any level of safety consciousness, I chose no. Now, I upset a client that day, and I have to admit I was partly to blame. The mistake I made was to create an expectation in my client's mind that the group *would* climb the high elements (because this is what I said would happen). Yet, upon witnessing their interactions up close, it was very clear that this was an unrealistic expectation. Since that day, I have chosen the words I use with clients more carefully, instead promising to use a variety of adventure-based activities in my programs, some of which *may* include the elements of a high challenge ropes course.

And thirdly, many a program has gone awry on the basis of an unrealistic (assumed) expectation that the group comes equipped with a supportive, productive and healthy culture. Ummm, no. Not often. Certainly not newly-formed groups, and rarely even among long-established, intact groups.

It is safer to assume that groups, generally, do not know how to behave in the most positive, supportive and productive manner. To this end, you are well advised to set some clearly defined expectations around what it means to be involved in your program. More on this in Part Three.

4. Poor Needs Analysis
or Not Knowing Whom You're Working With

This mistake should be self-explanatory. More often than not, if a program fails to achieve its objectives, a poor understanding of the client's needs is at the heart of the problem. A classic example…

In the midst of a busy month of programs, I chose to spend the time on my flight between Melbourne and Sydney to plan a last-minute program. The client called me only three days in advance, and we discussed all of the normal program parameters such as venue, numbers, goals, duration, etc. I picked up my rental car at the airport, tackled peak-hour traffic, and finally arrived at the venue with two minutes to spare. Then, as I swaggered into the reception area to enquire where I should be, I looked around and figured I must be in the wrong place because it had all the signs of an aged-care facility. Panicked, thinking I was now late, I turned to walk back to my car, when I heard my name. I was, in fact, at the right place. One very important question I forgot to ask was the age of the participants. An average of 80+ years. Hmm, I thought, there goes my three hours of 'high energy games' out the window.

In the world of realistic expectations, another shortfall of a poor needs analysis is the decision to commit to a shorter program than is (realistically) required, or to a program that lies outside of one's skill set.

If you want to do the very things that groups value about your work, then you must say No to opportunities that require more time or budget than your client is willing to give, or more skills than you can realistically offer. If you believe that you must keep your promises and meet your group's needs, this may mean suggesting follow-up sessions, or multi-day programs, or a decision to involve other professionals. Anything less is akin to handing your group a half-filled glass of water when they thirst for a full glass.

In Part Three, we'll look at what a thorough needs analysis looks like, and how it can help you to exceed your group's expectations.

the key to leading programs which are remarkably fun and meaningful is the type of environment you create ...

5. Not Valuing People's Time
or Wasting Opportunities

One of the biggest thieves of value in a program, any program, is permitting waste. The worst offender of them all is not starting on time, and this waste is all the more painful because it is totally avoidable.

An illustration. Let's say, your program starts at 9 am and finishes at 4 pm. Allowing for multiple breaks and lunch, you may be left with, say, 5.5 hours of actual program time. Multiply that by the number of people in your group multiplied by their respective pay scales (or the 'opportunity cost' of doing something else in the case of non-commercial programs), and you can expect the cost per minute to be extremely high. And yet, we permit people to show up late. Indeed, we build this waste into the program. Really? I don't get it.

Not only does delaying the 'official start' reward those who are late, but it punishes those who arrive on time. So, what's the message here? It's okay to show up late? An extremely costly mistake.

You only have to look at any university lecture hall to understand this mentality. The average student thinks, "Why turn up on time when the teacher will only wait for late-comers anyway?" It's a self-fulfilling prophecy because the teacher chooses to delay the start of his or her lecture to allow more time for students to arrive.

This rant is not about punctuality, or picking on people who, for all intents and purposes, are just being rude. No, I want to focus your attention elsewhere. More powerfully, I prefer to shift the responsibility for this waste onto me, the program leader.

I believe this all-too-common mistake presents an opportunity to add extra value, an opportunity we shall explore with many practical examples in Part Four.

6. Neglecting the Power of Story
or Our Brains Think in Pictures

How often have you related your fascination with the latest TV commercial to others, only to realise you can't recall the actual product being advertised? Such is the power of story.

As I look around, a very common mistake many program leaders make is to neglect the powerful medium of telling stories in their programs. They rely too heavily on their ability to articulate, or their charismatic personality, or worse, the presumption that their group will remember everything they say. Rarely do these skills alone stick the key messages of a program in the minds of people as powerfully and for as long as stories.

Stories are just one of the tools you can use to make a difference for your group, to help you do work that matters. In short, the absence of stories will stunt the power and enjoyment of your program.

Stories don't have to be humorous, but they should reflect a purpose aligned to your program. A well-placed story can open a gathering with a laugh, or illustrate a key point in your presentation, or set the scene for the delivery of what's coming next.

For example, consider my choice to use the imagery of a water pump in the desert at the start of this book. This suggestion alone will conjure in your mind most of the basic elements of the story I pitched, and with some further thought, how it connects to the purpose of this book.

I often coach participants in my training workshops to draw pictures of their experience, rather than write a lengthy step-by-step description of what happened, because the brain thinks in pictures not in words. This is why the process of 'mind-mapping' is so powerful, and why stories – which are effectively a series of images – work so well. Our memories of anything are made up of pictures, not words.

Here's an example. Elephant. Instantly, I can guarantee your mind will have retrieved the image of an elephant in your mind's eye and not the actual word. Or, consider the sketch of an elephant in your diary, for instance. The image will trigger a whole sequence of memories connected to your first elephant ride in India ten years ago, something you may not have thought of in years.

Stories are fun, they are powerful and in my experience, are not used as often as they should be, especially when people interact and respond to them so well. This is a mistake, and one that can be quickly overcome.

7. Absence of Fun or Flow
or What's In It For Me?

As mentioned earlier, if people can not see the 'fun' in an experience, they will find it very difficult to engage in your program. You could have everything else in order – you may have thoroughly analysed your group's needs, developed realistic expectations, started on time, etc – and yet, if you neglect to make the overall experience fun, your program will fail.

Now, when I say fun, I don't necessarily mean rolling around on the floor in fits of laughter. Don't get me wrong, this can be fun, but the fun I am particularly referring to is a level of engagement and general sense of enjoyment which nourishes one's soul or well-being. Yes, it may make you smile, but many more things beyond humour make you and I smile.

Time after time, I have sat through a boring presentation, or a threatening conference session or an awkward group interaction, and in all cases, I would argue no one was having any fun. These types of experiences will spoil any chance you have of creating a memorable and powerful group experience, i.e., to make a difference.

When you boil it down, having fun can be as simple as sharing an experience, any experience, in which you get lost in the 'flow.' Flow is a state of mind, much like the way Dr Stuart Brown, founder of the National Institute for Play, describes the properties of play – it is attractive, voluntary, purposeless, free of time and self-consciousness and you want it to last forever.

Going to the movies, engaging in a long in-depth conversation, playing sport (even when you lose), scaling a rock-climbing wall, starting a new enterprise – all of these experiences can be 'fun' because they involve many of the critical properties of flow.

While, there is no special formula, I will say that 'fun' and 'flow' will only occur when one critical element is present – a conducive environment.

There must be choice, people must feel valued, opportunities for challenge and growth are possible, and most important of all, there must be some form of interaction – with oneself, others and / or the environment.

Let's be honest – how many of these elements are truly present in your program?

If there is one thing I want you to take away from this book, it's this: The key to leading programs which are remarkably fun and meaningful is the type of environment you create.

Our next chapter will explore a simple, yet very powerful model which reveals the secret to creating the most conducive type of programming environment, every time.

5

Zone of Proximal Development

"There has never been a meaningful life built on easy street."

– John Paul Warren, pastor

When you examine the most common mistakes that program leaders make, they all stem from the particular approach adopted, and hence the type of environment they create as a result. These types of environments are ineffective because they often serve to push people away, rather than encourage the sort of interactions which produce fun and meaningful outcomes.

So, let's spend a few minutes understanding the science behind what's going on here.

Introducing the Zone of Proximal Development

First of all, thank you for glancing at the title of this page, and continuing to read. Honestly, the title is the most difficult part of my message here. However, to be fair, this is the name given by the boffins to describe the fascinating process of how people (and therefore, groups) develop their skills.

So, what does the Zone of Proximal Development (or ZPD) process have to do with leading successful group programs and events?

Umm, in a word, everything. The extraordinarily simple, yet powerful model of the ZPD inspires and informs everything about a successful approach to program design and delivery. In short, embracing the technology of the ZPD will help set your group up for success.

Without getting too bogged down in the research and science, the ZPD is the difference between what a person can do without help and what he or she can do with help. It also distinguishes a zone in which a person can do little other than respond with fight or flight.

These developmental zones, which are just another name for environments, are illustrated below.

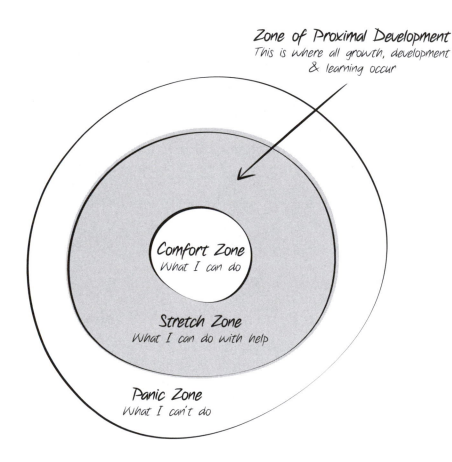

The theory of the ZPD, first developed by psychologist Lev Vygotsky (1896-1934), focused initially on a person's ability to solve a problem. However, over the years, this model has expanded broadly to include the development of all human competencies and skills. And, thus, its relevance to the development of interpersonal skills.

If the number one element which must be present for your program to be successful is an environment conducive to having fun and developing high quality interaction, then we can apply this model to help us make this happen.

A Personal Illustration

In 2009, my wife and I spent a fantastic three months living in Florence, Italy. Before we arrived, we could speak only two words of Italian – spaghetti and Ferrari, which didn't get us very far.

We moved into an apartment in the 'old city,' and two days later, started an intensive four-week Italian language course. The goal at the end of our three month stay (apart from eat wonderful food, drink wine and travel extensively) was to be able to hold a basic conversation with Italians in their native tongue.

The course involved four hours of instruction every day, five days a week for four weeks. Talk about full-on... barely an English word was uttered during the classes. Within a couple of days, we were practically crumpled up in the corner, rocking back and forth, mumbling something about what the hell are we doing here.

Let's refer to the ZPD model to explore what happened.

When given a choice, people almost always prefer to operate from within their 'comfort zones.' This is a bit like visiting Florence with an Italian phrase book in your pocket, but expecting everyone you meet will be able to speak a modicum of English.

Granted, the decision to simply visit a foreign country could push some people outside of their comfort zones, or perhaps, into their panic zones. However, for the purposes of this illustration, I am wanting to focus on the relationship between the zones, and its impact on developing positive forms of human interaction.

The Comfort zone is that area of competency which requires no external assistance or facilitation to perform. So, for the most part, as long as you do not stray too far off the tourist map, you will remain in your Comfort zone.

A Second Illustration

However, let's say that you choose to do some independent sight-seeing, and somehow end up in a village which very few tourists encounter. Not only have you forgotten your phrase book, but very few locals in this village know or speak English. Uh-oh. You now enter the Stretch zone.

Sitting down at a restaurant table, you are now faced with the challenge of reading the menu, and communicating your need, let's say, for a gluten-free meal. After several halting conversations with an elderly waiter, the help of the young bartender is enlisted to translate your needs. In the language of the ZPD, this is classic development within the Stretch zone because it requires assistance, i.e., you could not communicate "gluten-free" on your own.

As a further distinction, this experience would not be regarded as occurring within the Panic zone because the assistance which was offered was all that was necessary to return you closer to your Comfort zone (insofar as your Comfort zone has grown to include 'how to say gluten-free').

Having learned the Italian phrase for 'gluten-free,' you would now be equipped to order many more meals at other establishments. However, if no one could have understood your needs at this first restaurant, the situation could have easily moved into the Panic zone, because the only sensible option would have been to leave (flight).

Returning now, to my wife and I rocking back and forth in the corner. We were in our Panic zones, no doubt about it. Given our starting point, no level of assistance was going to prevent a disaster in the first week, so we were faced with a decision – fight or flight? We chose fight. We stuck with it, trusted the process and re-assessed our expectations, i.e., maybe we shouldn't expect to speak like an Italian on the third day of the course. We were now comfortably back in the Stretch zone. Not our Comfort zone, mind you, because this would have meant giving up our three month goal. No, instead, we chose to be challenged (stretched) every day, but we were a lot gentler on ourselves and agreed that we would take it one day, and one conversation, at a time.

For the record, we did achieve our goal, admirably. Between my penchant for 'grammatica' and my wife's excellent 'pronuncia' skills, we had many productive conversations in Italian with lots of locals, including a policeman who had arrested us for fare-evasion, but that's another story…

all learning occurs in the Stretch zone …

Zone Implications

While simple in nature, there are some important implications you must consider to broaden your understanding of the ZPD:

- All learning occurs in the Stretch zone, only.

- Learning does not occur in the Comfort zone because no assistance is required; that is, you have everything you need to accomplish the task, or solve the problem, successfully. Learning does not occur in the Panic zone either, other than perhaps learning never to return to that space again (think, cat on a hot stove top).

- The primary role of education is to invite people into their Stretch zones.

- If education is the purpose of your program, then how you do this is the million dollar question. There are many methods, some better than others. The methodology described in this book focuses on a very attractive, powerful and universally applicable method. More on this shortly.

- There exist at least two types of zones – individual and group.

- While the focus of this book is on groups of people, it must be acknowledged that each individual has his or her own distinct ZPD. That is, to say, what stretches one person may fit completely within the Comfort zone of another, or indeed, the outer extremities of the Panic zone for someone else.

- The challenge, of course, as with all group work, is to design a program which meets the needs of all of the people in your group as much as possible. A neat trick when this happens.

- Within a zone, there are varying degrees of comfort, stretch and panic.

- Graphically, it is easy to understand the different degrees to which you can experience comfort, stretch and panic. The closer one gets to the very centre of the circle, the more comfortable (less stretched or panicked) one becomes. And vice versa. Naturally, it always 'depends on the situation.'

Exploring What Went Wrong

To bed this knowledge down, let's apply the ZPD model to explore each of the seven most common mistakes to a series of actual, real-life programs.

1. Not Breaking the Ice

Situation: One minute into his training session, an instructor invites each person to stand up and introduce themselves, starting with the person to his left, moving clockwise around the room. The first person barely looks up at the group when she speaks, the second person passes, etc.

Impact: We've all been in this situation. In a word, horrible. While there will always be one or two who will cherish their moment in the spotlight (their personal Comfort zone), most people are pushed into the outer edges of their Stretch zone, if not, their Panic zone when asked to talk in front of others. Too much too soon. Most people list public-speaking as their number one fear, and dislike it even more when they have to talk about themselves. Epic fail.

2. Lack of Philosophical Framework

Situation: A class of students attends a three-day camp, during which they participate in a variety of 'team-building' initiatives designed to help them function better at school. Most of the activities deteriorate into a farce. The students divide into two groups – those who want to do the activities, and those who would sooner play video games on their bunk.

Impact: It is possible that a lack of purpose and buy-in from the students at the start pushed many of them outside of their Comfort zones, and they did not receive the assistance they needed to learn from this experience. Some students, already challenged by the nature of a few of the camp activities, do not feel 'safe' or valued, so they preferred to shut-down (Panic zone) than participate. An unmitigated disaster which, sadly, only reinforced what was happening back at school.

3. Unrealistic Expectations

Situation: A half-day conference has been urgently scheduled to discuss and develop the one, three and five-year action plans for the organisation. The facilitator pushes the group hard to make many decisions within the allotted time. Some staff come away from the meeting feeling railroaded.

Impact: Apart from the obvious case of asking for too much in too little time, there may also be a case to answer for how prepared the staff were to contribute with such short notice. None of this experience lands within the team's Comfort zone, and was unsupported in their Stretch zone. It is highly likely that most of the decisions were made within a Panic zone mentality, i.e., let's just get it done.

4. Poor Needs Analysis

Situation: A group of teachers is required to attend a professional development course to study the fine art of horse-whispering, two days before school starts. There are tears, arguments and two teachers leave early in disgust.

Impact: Maybe the experience of young colts surrounded by a group of adults holding hands in a circle is similar to how students feel on the first day of school, but really? The teacher's minds are so focused on other more pressing (professional) needs, not to mention the very real prospect of being hurt by a large, powerful animal, this clearly pushed people into their Panic zones. There was no choice, no apparent purpose. This was headed for mis-adventure from the get-go.

5. Not Valuing People's Time

Situation: An annual conference attracts hundreds of professionals from around the globe. The convenor waits until everyone has registered and entered the auditorium before starting. While waiting, some people leave the auditorium to make a quick phone call, or visit the bathroom, only exacerbating the issue. The keynote speaker is required to cut her presentation in half to keep to the schedule.

Impact: Even if we can accept the loss of value from squeezing a one hour keynote presentation into 30 minutes, two very real costs are apparent. The bore of sitting quietly in a half-filled auditorium two seats away from anyone else (typical Comfort zone behaviour, i.e., no growth), and the opportunity cost of not leveraging this idle time to generate energy, warmth and relationships. Certainly, the keynote speaker would have appreciated this, and thousands of dollars are wasted in time and international airfares.

6. Neglecting the Power of Story

Situation: A weekly youth group meeting dedicates 30 minutes of their evening to a bible study. This week, the local pastor is invited to share her understanding of a particular parable. She directs questions to the whole group, to gauge comprehension, but very few people respond.

Impact: All else being equal, the issue here is a lack of story. The young people are quite capable of exploring the issue at hand, but they struggle to connect the abstract lessons on the slide presentation to their lives (a task stranded on the outer edges of their Stretch zone, again, without assistance). Disengaged, most of the young people are lost in other thoughts within five minutes. They also reel at the risk of responding to a topic they do not understand in front of the whole group (Panic zone). Disappointing loss of potential.

7. Absence of Fun

Situation: On the first day of the school year, a PE teacher notices there are many new students who have joined her class. First up, she decides to run a series of games to mix everyone up. After an energetic hour of activity, three distinct cliques appear – the athletic kids, the not-so-cool kids and the new kids.

Impact: While there may have been lots of activity with good intentions, the program failed in two significant ways – while physically oriented, the activities were not fun, nor socially interactive. Indeed, many games actively eliminated kids. Many students retreated into their shells (classic Panic zone stuff) because they feared being picked on, in some cases, again. Classic dysfunction.

Incidentally, we'll return to each of these situations in Part Four to explore some simple and practical solutions.

What Does All This Mean?

So, what can the ZPD teach us about leading programs that are fun and meaningfully connected to the lives of our groups? There are five key learnings:

- By default, people are programmed to function from within their Comfort zones, that space which is familiar and keeps them safe. This is the domain of so-so. People sitting next to people they know. Keeping quiet rather than speaking up and looking foolish. Arriving late because this is easier than accepting responsibility for being on time, and so on.

- Growth and development only occur in the Stretch zone, where people require some level of assistance or guidance to fulfil their potential. This is the domain of awesome. People and groups operating within this zone are kicking goals. It's not always easy, they often need help, but they achieve so much more.

- The more often people are invited to step willingly into their Stretch zones, the bigger their Comfort zones get because they absorb a small part of their old Stretch zone. In your efforts to create a truly powerful and engaging environment for interaction, this (growing) process should be one of your primary goals.

- Push people too far, and they will enter their Panic zones and retreat, act out or simply shut down. Look no further than the seven mistakes we have discussed so far.

These are the consequences of not acknowledging people's Comfort zones – that is, an environment which is conducive to fun and positive interaction – and expecting anything else will only cause you trouble.

• You must give people a reason to step outside of their Comfort Zones, otherwise, they won't budge. Remember, environment dictates performance. This principle alone explains why many programs meet resistance and fail to achieve their fullest potential. If your group is not ready, they will not be prepared to stretch, yet.

Making A Difference

If you truly want to make a difference – to shift the experience of your program from so-so to awesome – you are obliged to invite your group to move out of their Comfort zones. This shift requires a higher level of interaction, and typically, your group needs your help to do this because they can't (or won't) do it on their own.

Did you get that? Your group needs you to help them.

Unaware that they are stuck, your group members are quite comfortable sitting in their Comfort zones, so they do not perceive any need for help. But, if they are to consider stepping out of their Comfort zones, you need to give them a very good reason to do so.

And the most powerful reason to achieve this goal is ... fun

As I consider how I do what I do, by far the most potent tool I employ is fun. Fun, taken seriously, is the key. It answers the 'What's in it for me?' question everybody is asking.

Fun is the carrot I dangle in front of people to encourage them to step outside of their Comfort zones, to experience the value of 'stretching' a little. It is the thread which weaves in and out of my methodology, a topic we are now ready to explore.

by far the most potent
tool I employ is fun ...

part three
PUMP

Pumping Like Crazy

"We are what we repeatedly do.
Excellence then, is not an act, but a habit."
– Aristotle, philosopher

No one sets out to be average. In fact, we all want to be the exact opposite. I want to do work that matters, that is fun and has meaning, and I expect that you do too.

Yet, as I pondered the question, how do I do what I do after twenty-five years, I just put it down to intuition. Fun was a huge factor, but how could I share what came to me naturally? And then, I understood – intuition is just unexplored process.

Here's what I also discovered – my process is not about *being* different, it's about *creating* a difference.

To 'be different' is to say I have more experience, more charisma, more tools, more whatever, all of which only aim to dominate the market place for my skills. The focus of *being different* is on me.

To 'create a difference' is doing work that matters – for you, your group and the world. Creating a difference in the way people come together that changes the way they feel, leads to the creation of more fun and more meaning in their lives. The focus of *creating a difference* is on my group.

This is what I care about. This is my process.

The pages that follow explore the tools I use and the steps I take to create remarkably fun programs. Then, and only then, can I inspire and equip my groups to do work that matters to them.

... to create a difference is to do work that matters

6

The Tools

"A tradesman is only as good as his tools."

– author unknown

A carpenter looks at a piece of lumber and can see a finely crafted table. A potter casts her eye over a messy lump of clay, and yet, can see an ornate vase. A writer stares at an empty screen, but imagines a book.

As a program leader, I see a group of people longing to connect, to be noticed, to matter. They want to know that what they are about to do makes sense and has meaning to their group, their professions, their lives.

There are tools essential to the creative process. My particular craft is practised with tools you cannot see, but will be largely felt.

You see, it is impossible to change how people think or what they do without, first, changing how they feel. These are the tools I use to influence the way people feel...

First and foremost is fun. It is my most potent tool.

Like detergent mixed with oil, fun has the greatest power to cut through the crap. It promotes interaction and frames the use of each of the other four essential tools. There's no accident that they happen to align with my four-step methodology:

1. **Goals (Plan)** – setting clear expectations and the reasons for meeting them.

2. **Choice (Prime)** – the ability to choose if, when and how far one may step outside their comfort zone.

3. **Full Value (Pump)** – an agreement which frames and adds value to a group's interactions.

4. **Reflection (Peak)** – a process which enables the discovery of learning and growth.

Together, they form the cornerstones of the adventure-based learning model, particularly as adopted by Project Adventure's innovative approach to experiential programming.

The following sections describe each one of these five tools in more detail. Together, when used with care, they create an environment which will generate:

- Satisfaction – surprising levels of fun and enjoyment which invite even more participation.

- Community – you will break the ice, build trust and strengthen relationships.

- Support and Empathy – a heightened level of interaction which develops social and emotional learning skills.

- Significance – your program will have meaning and relevance for your group.

What will making a difference mean to your group?

FUNN

"Fun does not come in sizes."

– Bart Simpson, cartoon character

Obvious fun is very hard to stand away from. It's contagious and pretty much speaks everyone's language. Fun disarms people, because it often involves a lot of unself-conscious activity. And, let's face it – it's hard to look cool when everyone else is having a great time.

I'm sure you noted the misspelling, but there's no mistake. FUNN is a whimsical acronym which means Functional Understanding Not Necessary, a term coined by the masterful Karl Rohnke that says "If it's fun, I want to be a part of it." Which is exactly its purpose.

FUNN is good, agreeable, contagious, its own reward, etc, etc, but it will also help to facilitate your program goals. The beauty is that your group does not need to know that this is happening, i.e., functional understanding is not necessary. Yet, programmatically, a liberal dose of fun is absolutely essential if you want to influence the way people feel, and create an environment which encourages them to step outside their Comfort zones.

FUNN greases the wheels of interaction and invites people to laugh, share, play, loosen up, set the tone, change the pace, and so on – all of which contribute manifestly to the breaking of ice and the strengthening of trust and relationships.

An illustration. I always, always, always, pull out a 'minute-mover' (simple, quick energiser) at the very start of a program to engage my audience quickly, and get them laughing and, perhaps, interacting. Sometimes, I connect the exercise to the theme of the day, or simply invite everyone to enjoy the spectacle. Conference organisers and keynote speakers love me for this trick alone. There is nothing better than entering a space which has been warmed up, and exudes a strong sense of everybody leaning in and ready to go.

Fun. Never leave home without it.

… fun is absolutely essential
if you want to influence the
way people feel

Goal-Setting

"The journey of a thousand miles begins with one step."
– Lao Tzu, philosopher

The process of setting goals, and working towards them, is very clearly and unquestionably beneficial to your program.

Research has repeatedly shown that groups achieve more when they set a goal, because goals motivate people as much as guide and direct their energy towards a common objective.

Setting goals is more than just facing everyone in the same direction, though. It's about giving people a reason to participate especially if their (or your program) goal sits outside of their Comfort zone. To this end, it is particularly powerful to involve your group in the goal-setting process (if possible) because this choice will give them more control of, and allow them to feel more responsible for, the final result.

Goals can be explicit or implicit, casual or very formal. They are the lens through which every exercise and interaction should be viewed as you design and deliver your program.

Short programs – such as conferences and business meetings – tend to adopt very simple, often implicit goals, whereas longer programs – such as a classroom, the development of a healthy organisational culture and weekly youth group meetings – always benefit from investing more time and effort to the process.

SMART Goals

A poor process to setting an effective goal, or worse, the absence of a goal, are two of the main reasons programs fail. In my goal-setting endeavours, I have found it useful to follow the SMART goal guidelines to set effective goals. SMART goals are:

S **Specific** – clear and concise, one goal at a time

M **Measurable** – in time and quantity

A **Achievable** – realistic, but also a stretch

R **Relevant** – has direct significance and connection

T **Trackable** – allows monitoring of progress

Here's a great example of the impact of setting an effective goal.

A group of dysfunctional young people were forced to attend a weekend camp. Following a series of high-energy, fun activities, my colleagues and I helped the young people set two SMART goals. In their own words, their most immediate goal was to 'go back home,' which, in time, we could promise would be achieved. However, we worked with them to set a second goal – to have fun. This had all the hallmarks of a SMART goal – specific, easy to measure, was certainly achievable and was trackable. But the key to its success was the R, relevance – this goal mattered to the young people because the alternative was to endure a miserable couple of days before they could achieve their first goal. This second goal framed every interaction and conversation we had from that point on. There is no doubt, that without this second goal, we would have been butting heads all weekend.

Later, in the first step of my methodology (Plan), we will expand on the technology of SMART goals to learn a very powerful method for setting goals that makes a difference. This method expands on the R factor – relevance – and will make all the difference to your group.

Challenge By Choice

"One could always point to a time. A choice.
An act that set the tone for a life
and changed a personal destiny."

– Carol O'Connell, author

None of us enjoy being forced or coerced to do something we don't want to do. Even when these 'things' are good for me, an approach which gives me the power to choose will always be more successful than feeling under pressure to participate because of some threatening external factor, such as my peers, the boss, a teacher, etc.

Remember, you can't change the way people think or act until you have changed the way they feel. Recognising that authentic change comes from within, this tool creates an environment within which people can feel comfortable to make decisions consistent with, and appropriate to, the overall goals of your program. In short, it helps interactions flow.

A term first coined by Karl Rohnke (and later popularised by Project Adventure), Challenge by Choice is a powerful programming tool which states that people have the choice to determine their own level of involvement in any given activity. Nobody is, or should be coerced to do anything they don't want to do.

Notice then, that Challenge by Choice shifts the responsibility onto you, the program provider, to create a space which encourages your group's participation.

Or, in other words, to create a space within which people can step outside their Comfort zones into their Stretch zones. This is exactly as it should be, and not the other way around.

Yet, if you take a good look around, you'll discover a disturbingly different picture. I have seen and been a part of too many programs which do nothing to foster a supportive environment, and just expect people to participate. Once again, some program leaders wonder why they meet resistance.

More Than Just Saying 'No'

However, embracing this tool as a core theme of your programming approach is more than simply allowing your participants to say "No" and pull out of an activity.

Challenge by Choice allows people to pull back from a challenge that may push them into their Panic zone, and rather than pull out, invites them to find another role (hopefully within their Stretch zone) that works for them. You could call this a Challenge *of* Choice, whereby someone chooses their level of challenge.

For example, someone may prefer not to be physically carried across the 'peanut-butter' pit as part of a team-building exercise, but is willing to participate in the gentler problem-solving process. Or, rather than address the whole class, each student is invited to share their response with a small group.

When you are profoundly related to this powerful concept of choice, it will permeate every aspect of your program design and delivery. It's the difference between "You have to..." and "You are invited to..." Or "If you make a mistake, you have to come into the centre of the circle..." and "If you're not quick enough, it's your turn to have some fun in the centre..."

Perhaps you already embrace this concept in your program. Fantastic. But note, it's one thing to say "...this program operates under the philosophy of Challenge by Choice..." It's entirely another thing to be responsible for a program that speaks to, honours and fosters an atmosphere in which people genuinely feel comfortable to willingly step outside of their Comfort zone.

A Word on Participation

Many people – program leaders and participants alike – often confuse Challenge by Choice with 'participation.' This is a simple trap. A case in point...

Many years ago, I trained a team of police instructors to deliver a program which purposefully mixed police recruits with groups of 'youth at risk.' To be honest, I'd be hard-pressed to think of two more diametrically opposed groups. By mid-morning of the first day, the program was humming along nicely, however, two of the young people chose not to join in. As a part of the facilitation team, I respected their decision to sit out, but I did take it somewhat personally because I could not see any reasons why they should choose to not join in. Ignoring even the urgings of their friends, nothing it seemed could motivate these two girls to participate. By day's end, the two girls did not move from their comfortable sidelined position. And then, it happened. To wrap up the day, the top brass of the police squadron asked the group a few questions, a debrief of sorts, including the stock-standard "What did you learn about each other today?" To my shock, one of the two girls put up her hand. I'm thinking, "What smart-arse comment are you going to make? You didn't participate all day." She replied something to the effect, "I didn't think the coppers would laugh at the same things we did!" And then it hit me. This girl had been participating all day; she just chose (for whatever reason) to do it from the sidelines. It was one of those 'aha' moments we all strive for, and was only made possible because of the atmosphere that had been developed during the day, particularly enabled by the use of Challenge by Choice. If this girl had been forced to participate, I am certain that the result would have been very different. The girls joined the rest of the group on the second day, and had a blast.

Full Value Contract

"The best way to predict the future is to create it."
– Abraham Lincoln, US President

If Challenge by Choice acknowledges that people tend to enter into a new experience from within their Comfort zones, the Full Value Contract is the vehicle that they can use to arrive safely at the other end.

In the context of creating powerful spaces within which people can interact, the Full Value Contract is all about keeping this space as fun as possible, as much as keeping it as 'safe' as possible.

All people have a right to be valued, and valuing oneself is as important as valuing others. Accordingly, the Full Value Contract creates a coherent, shared and conscious understanding (or agreement) about how people are expected to behave. To not focus on this critical notion, is akin to driving without a seat-belt – the longer the drive, the greater the chance of an accident.

You see, the longer people spend together, the more comfortable they become with one another. Slowly, their interactions move into the Stretch zone, and, it is at this point, we need more than just good intentions to keep things moving smoothly. As with all things in the Stretch zone, your group will need assistance.

What Is It?

The Full Value Contract is a device (much like a seat-belt) that helps individuals and groups to achieve their program goals in a safe and supportive environment. No matter what group or program you care to mention – from a weekly youth group meeting to multi-day, team-building workshops – every program will benefit from the process of consciously defining what is expected of people's behaviours.

That said, programs which involve the same people over a long period of time – such as schools, corporate and community organisations – need and benefit from the structure offered by a Full Value Contract significantly more than shorter, one-off programs. Longer programs have more opportunities to develop the hidden potential of the group, and therefore, achieve mightier and more challenging goals.

The Full Value Contract is the cornerstone of Project Adventure's work and has many and varied forms. It may be written or oral, explicit or implicit, casual or formal. No matter what shape it takes, it is a shared creation, and should embrace three broad tasks:

1. To understand and create safe behavioural norms under which the group will operate;

2. Seek a commitment to adhere to these norms by everyone in the group; and

3. To accept a shared responsibility for the maintenance of the group.

Importantly, the Full Value Contract ought to fit the unique goals, characteristics and spirit of your group. Therefore, the shape of the Full Value Contract you develop for a one-hour basketball clinic with children will differ significantly from that created for a residential therapy group for adults. So will the agreement formed between adjudicated youth and that developed for a one-day professional conference.

At one end of the spectrum, the way you lead your program and interact with your group will communicate implicitly what is expected. At the other extreme, you may have to instruct everyone to sign a contract which explicitly states what is and is not appropriate behaviour.

With clearly defined boundaries, people know where they stand and comfortably make decisions about the type and level of their involvement. The more ambiguous these boundaries are, the less inclined your group will be to interact outside of their Comfort zone.

Why Bother?

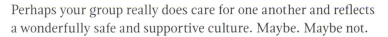

every program will benefit from the process of consciously defining what is expected of people's behaviours ...

All fine and dandy, you might say, but why bother?

Perhaps your group really does care for one another and reflects a wonderfully safe and supportive culture. Maybe. Maybe not.

Most groups, no matter the reason for their existence or length of program, will benefit from some form of 'conversation' which aims to guide their behaviours, ultimately, to leverage their fullest potential. Even groups that have been together for a long time – such as a school class, or a work-team – will gain a lot from the process of sharing and making conscious those aspects of their collective norms that are acceptable, and those that are not.

In my experience, much of the discussion reflects typically unwritten, unspoken laws of 'how we do things around here.' Naturally, for those groups that are just forming, or will only gather for a short time, there is no such thing and will start with a clean slate.

Even if the list of 'norms' is exactly the same for every member of the group, the process of actually sharing and making this agreement a conscious one benefits everybody. It will set your group up for success, because its potential will not get bogged down in petty grievances and misunderstandings further down the track.

Turn to Part Four to acquaint yourself with a variety of Full Value Contract designs to get you started.

Experiential Learning Cycle

"People will believe more in knowledge
they have discovered themselves
than in knowledge presented by others."

– David Johnson & Roger Johnson, psychologists

If education or professional development is one of your program goals, this next tool will become one of your most powerful allies.

There is a lot of evidence to suggest that learning happens most effectively in a four-step process, and adopting this process will help your program – in whole or in part – become a more valuable and meaningful experience for everyone.

The Experiential Learning Cycle (ELC), developed by David Kolb, is an 'action-reflection' model, and one of the foundations of adventure education. Refer to the diagram overleaf.

The ELC will give you a structure to follow in your work as you seek to draw more meaning or learning from your program. It proposes that the transfer of learning will be more effective if what is being learned is discovered though actual experience or, as it is sometimes referred to, 'learning by doing.'

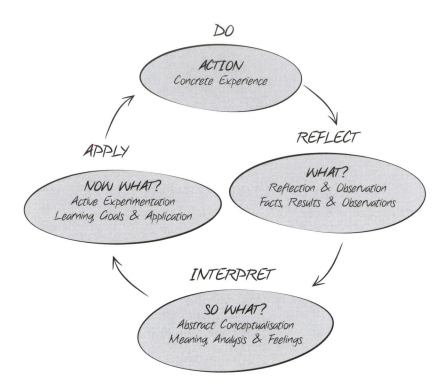

However, the practice of simply 'doing' does not, in and of itself, create 'learning.' If your program is all about having fun, then this 'hands-off' approach may be fine. But, if you are looking to have a more substantive impact, you are well advised to 'facilitate' the learning process.

This process, also known as a debrief, review or reflection, is an opportunity for your group to process what has been learned from a particular experience. Guided by a series of questions which you pose, your group can talk things out and tackle relevant issues, such as communication and leadership within the group.

Within the context of a safe and supportive atmosphere (perhaps governed by a Full Value Contract), they can also provide feedback to one another and raise significant learning points.

Obviously, this is higher-order, Stretch Zone stuff. Adopting the action-reflection model of the ELC means that your group can not expect to be fed the answers, so there's work to be done. Starting small and building up over time, you can expect your group to continue to improve, testing the limits of their self-perceived boundaries.

To work effectively, this process works hand-in-hand with each of the other tools, especially Goal-Setting, Challenge by Choice and the Full Value Contract.

How to Debrief

As I talk with others, many program leaders feel the least confident or competent in their ability to process an experience compared to their other leadership skills. Fair enough too, because we tend to put a lot of pressure on ourselves to trawl for pearls of wisdom every time we debrief our groups.

Relax. Volumes have been written about the art and science of processing, and they pretty much all boil down to four simple steps:

1. **The Doing** – the action or concrete experience.

2. **What?** – reflecting on the facts of 'what happened' in the experience.

3. **So What?** – generalising these facts, making connections and looking for patterns.

4. **Now What?** – applying this learning to the next experience, or ultimately, to people's real lives – at school, home, work and play.

Take a look at Part Four to read more details about the ELC and many practical tips to help you conduct effective debriefs.

7

The Methodology

"Success is a science;
if you have the conditions, you get the result."
– Oscar Wilde, writer

The Difference Model

Just as the man in the desert story had to trust the note and be patient to get at the promised water, you have finally arrived at the point in the book where I describe the four steps of my programming model.

To be fair, you have most of what you need to know to create an outrageously fun, interactive experience which will set your group up for success. But, there is just one wholly significant element left to describe – the sequence, or the progression of steps to follow.

Looking back, I wish this sequence, this series of steps, was shared with me when I first started out. For the most part, despite or in spite of my green, dewy-eyed approach, I kind of just figured it out. I noticed that when I followed a particular sequence, the program worked and my groups left feeling engaged, inspired and successful.

Of course, when I did not follow this sequence, the wheels would inevitably fall off somewhere along the way.

Over the years, I have referred to these steps a thousand times in my training workshops, and with each re-telling, refined them just a little to reflect more truthfully how I do what I do.

These are the four steps I take:

1. **Needs Analysis (Plan)** – working out the difference I am going to make.

2. **Setting the Tone (Prime)** – creating a fun, safe and supportive environment to invite interaction.

3. **Doing the Work (Pump)** – developing the level of engagement and skills to promote growth.

4. **The Difference (Peak)** – leveraging my group's potential to do work that matters.

The sections which follow describe these steps in detail, together with many useful leadership insights and examples.

These steps, and so much more, are modelled and explored more deeply in my training workshops.

Step 1 – Plan Needs Analysis

"Make it about them, not about you."

– Simon Sinek, author

This first critical step is not a guessing game, nor should it be regarded as more important than anything else. But, it does lay an important foundation for the success of your program.

The Plan or Needs Analysis step is the note hidden under the rock by Desert Pete. If the note is not found, or the desert traveller chooses not to follow its instructions, we're unlikely to see a 'happily ever after' ending to the story.

While clearly not a matter of life and death for you and me, the allegory reminds us that this step must always be the first task we undertake before we walk out in front of our group.

To my mind, everything about this step points to one critical question:

What Difference are You Going to Make?

This question is not asking how or why are you different to, say, another teacher, or corporate trainer or Scout leader, etc. The question I challenge you to answer is – what difference is your program going to make in the life of your group, and how will it make them feel? From their perspective.

Right off the bat, this is a tough question, because most program leaders think only in terms of goals and not what they want their group to *become*.

But, I remind you why we are here – to make a difference. Yes, you want to deliver a wonderfully fun, interactive program, but what happens next? The Difference Model deliberately starts with difference and ends with difference.

Let's imagine Desert Pete, for a moment, undertaking a needs analysis of his hypothetical water supply program. In our story, he decides that the difference he is going to make is to promise an unlimited supply of water for every desert traveller. As we know from his plan (the note), a lot of risk and work is attached to this promise. Yet, in a parallel universe, Pete could have been tempted to take a short-cut, and just direct people to the bottle under the rock, or drink the water in the bottle himself and instruct everyone to an easier pump two sand dunes away.

In each case, there is a goal – to supply water. In each case, Desert Pete achieves this goal – but note, only one course of action makes a real difference to the life of a desert traveller.

This impact is what this first step – our needs analysis – is all about.

Anyone can set goals. Your task is to understand what the real needs of your group are, and to choose a course of action that will make a real difference to them.

Plan to Make a Difference

Let's get stuck into the three steps of planning.

1. Logistics
2. Apparent Goal
3. Difference

You'll find a template for this critical first step at the end of the chapter.

1. Logistics

If you're like me, faced with a choice of homework assignments, you always pick the easy ones first, right? Therefore, my planning always starts with the simple logistics of my program.

This level of planning is not rocket science, but for the less experienced among us, let's be more specific. You want to answer six basic questions:

- **When?** – on what date and time does the program run, and what breaks need to be scheduled?
- **Who?** – how many people are involved, and what is their demographic profile, e.g., age, experience, occupation, background, etc?
- **What?** – what is the context in which the program will be delivered, e.g., weekly meeting, annual conference, one-off, urgent, etc?
- **Where?** – where will the program be delivered, the physical environment (indoors, outdoors) and the amount of space available to use, e.g., gymnasium, classroom, community hall, fixed theatre-style seating, etc?
- **How?** – in what format does the group expect the program to be delivered, e.g., oral presentation, experiential, online, blended learning, etc.?

These questions should not take too long to complete. The more important work – answering the sixth question, Why? – demands more time and effort, and is developed across the next two steps.

2. Apparent Goal

There is always an apparent goal – the one staring you and your group in the face. It is often captured in the initial conversation you have (with yourself, or others) when you first consider your group's needs.

It may sound like... to have fun ... to build team skills ... to energise and wake up the group ... to develop leadership skills ... to prepare the group for X ... to fill in time ... to open the conference, and so on.

Your task at this point is to plug these brief responses into the SMART goal-setting model (refer to page 70) to set an effective goal.

... i remind you why you are here
— to make a difference

That is, while 'improving leadership skills' is an admirable goal, it is not particularly effective because it does not meet the useful characteristics of a SMART goal.

Here's a good example of a SMART goal that has been developed for a three-hour 'get-to-know-you' session for a group of new employees: Everyone will recall at least two things about ten other people by the end of the session.

This goal is SMART because it is (S) focused on one clearly defined goal, (M) measured in terms of people, recall and time, (A) will stretch the capabilities of the team, (R) important because it will fast-track the development of a new project team, and (T) by the end of the session, the team will know if the goal was achieved, or not.

Now, having answered the Why? question, this is the point where most program leaders conclude their goal-setting process.

This is a start, and there is nothing wrong with choosing to stop here. You have a goal, and this is better than not having a goal. But, having a goal is not the same as making a difference.

3. Difference

The R of the SMART goal-setting model points to a little of the depth required of this final planning step. It asks the Why? behind the Why?

You can't make a difference without, first, understanding why this difference will matter to your group. Once again, recalling a simple truth – you cannot change how people think or what they do without, first, changing how they feel.

This part of your needs analysis aims to go deeper, to a level which, once tapped, will unlock the true value of your program and more successfully engage your group on their journey with you. This is the kicker. When you nail this 'difference,' you'll be able to identify precisely how your program will leave your group feeling.

There is no set formula, simply an enquiry.

Here are two tools you can use to drill down deeper.

The Five Whys

This is a simple problem-solving technique that helps you get to the root of a problem quickly. Most often, the answer to the first Why? will prompt another Why? and the answer to the second question will prompt another Why? and so on.

Ask questions such as:

- Why does your group want to achieve this goal?
- Why is this important?
- Why does this matter, and to whom?

To illustrate: A corporation approaches me to deliver a 'team-building' workshop. I ask why? The manager tells me the company wants to build trust and develop stronger relationships among its staff. Why is this important? One particular team does not work well together, and they are relatively unproductive. Why does that matter? Many of the team members are unhappy at work, and the team is losing money. Why are they unhappy? As a team, they don't feel valued. Ahhhh, got it. You can now see what matters to this team. They do not feel that their work is being valued, and this is affecting their performance, not to mention the bottom-line of the company.

Fix how people are feeling, and you're on a winner. But more than this – everything about my approach with this team will be focused on making a difference: helping them to feel valued, empowered and satisfied at work. This will give them a reason to care about my training, and most importantly, to engage fully with it.

Notice, this plan is very different from the initial (apparent) goal of 'team-building.' Building a strong team would have been nice, but not enough to make a difference.

Empathy Enquiry

This technique will give you the ability to understand an experience as viewed through the eyes of your group. It will help you to explore why people do what they do, and build empathy for how they think and how they behave.

Ask questions such as:

- Why does your group exist – what is its purpose?
- What does your group believe?
- What does your group value?
- What is the world-view of your group?
- What do the people in your group care about?
- What feelings does your group often experience?
- What do the people in your group really want?

An example. A group of young people are sent out of school to a special two-hour class each week to improve their dysfunctional behaviours (apparent goal). In advance, the program leader spends a bit of time getting to know the boys, and identifies that the boys love taking risks, they care what their friends think about them, and they believe every teacher hates them. Over many weeks, the program, which involves lots of challenging, physical and adventurous activities, develops enough trust that the boys start to open up and share what's going on for them. Slowly, feeling listened to, some of the boys return to the mainstream classroom. The difference? To help the boys restore their self-esteem and take responsibility for their lives.

Once again, a plan which is very different to the apparent goal.

Exceeding Expectations

Often, your plan or needs analysis, will result in a statement of feeling, i.e., how it intends to leave your group feeling. In the two cases described above, the unproductive team leaves my program feeling valued and empowered, while the dysfunctional boys feel more confident and in control of their lives.

This is how we exceed our group's expectations.

The process I have described goes beyond 'setting goals.' It has impact, because you asked more questions and were prepared to make a difference that matters to your group (i.e., it is felt).

Here are some more examples of Difference:

- Youth Group Meeting – help every young person feel like they belong, and are valued by others.
- Conference Opening – help every delegate feel comfortable to meet others.
- Summer Camp – help each camper feel responsible for the health of their cabin.
- Group Therapy – help each person feel that they are powerful in the face of adversity.
- Charity Organisation – help every volunteer feel that their contribution makes a difference.

What difference is your group looking for?

Focus of Your Leadership

It should be pretty clear that the singular focus of the Plan step is – your group. Never take your eyes off them, their needs, their wants and their desires.

While your group is not present yet, your leadership in developing a powerful and rewarding plan for them will, soon enough, be abundantly clear.

You will note that as your program develops through each of the three remaining steps, your leadership role will change with each step.

Practical Plan Considerations

Now, remember, we have only ticked off the first of four steps of my programming model. But, before we move on, keep in mind the following thoughts:

- First, write your plan down. This simple task puts it into existence and helps you to be accountable.

- Your plan, much like a budget, is a starting point and not a straight jacket. Things will change, so expect to revise your plan as you go.

- Longer programs are sometimes more suited to this needs analysis process. Any process which takes longer than the actual program itself is probably not worth the trouble. That is not to say that short sessions do not benefit, but given the investment of time and effort, looking for 'difference' may be less useful.

- Always express your plan from your group's perspective. To 'help them feel confident' works better than 'to improve their confidence.'

- Be realistic. Ask yourself, what resources you need to help you make a difference? Are you the best person to lead the program? If not, then who can you involve?

- How will you know if you've made a difference, or reached your goals? What will it look like, sound like, feel like?

- Write your plan in the positive. For example, 'to help my group feel empowered,' rather than 'to eliminate disempowering thoughts and actions.'

- Stress-test your thoughts for making a difference with your group (or group leader). How do they respond? Does it speak to their issues?

PLAN: Needs Analysis Template

1. Logistics

When? Date and Time

Who?   Number and Demographic Profile

What?   Weekly, Annual, One-Off, Urgent

Where? Venue, Physical Environment, Space

How?   Format

2. Apparent Goal

Why?   Program objective(s)

Using SMART goal-setting guidelines, express in one sentence

3. Difference

Question: What difference are you going to make? How will this make your group feel? What do you want them to become?

Some questions to help you drill down deeper:

- Why does your group want to achieve this goal?
- Why is this important?
- Why does this matter, and to whom?
- Why does your group exist?
- What does your group believe?
- What does your group value?
- What do the people in your group care about?
- What do the people in your group really want?

Download your free copy of the Plan Template from
www.seriousfunbook.com

Step 2 – Prime
Setting The Tone

"It's fun to have fun, but you have to know how."

– Dr Suess, writer

You're standing in front of your group.

All eyes are on you. Everything hinges on your next move.

What do you do?

I love these moments, these feelings. It's this precise point when I can finally let go of any fears or stories I've been telling myself about what's going to happen, and shift my brain to finally focus on what I can make happen.

We are now ready to do something.

In the life of your group, or your program, everything up to this point is just fluff. Nothing has actually happened. All of the theories, framing and preparation in the world make not one iota of a difference to your group, until something actually happens.

Ordinarily, this is that part of the program when you pull out your 'ice- breakers,' right?

Wrong.

Guided by the needs analysis you performed in the first step, this second step is all about preparing your group – priming them – for the real work ahead. Get this step right – it's not hard, but it is critical – and everything which follows will be so much easier and significantly more successful, for you and your group.

This step sets the tone and begins the sensitive process of purposefully 'breaking the ice' and switching on people's brains. Recognising their proclivity for starting from within their Comfort zones, this step is not about playing 'ice-breaker' games as much as it is focused on breaking the ice.

Prime to Make a Difference

Involving only experiences which feature fun, simple, non-threatening and success-oriented interaction, here are the four steps which break the ice:

1. Unofficial Start
2. Official Start
3. Small Interaction
4. Bigger Interaction

You'll find a template for this second step at the end of the chapter.

Breaking the Ice

Having fun and making a difference is not just noticed – it's experienced and felt.

Ask for too much too soon – by not removing the ice – and you'll frighten your group away. But, progress too slowly – by neglecting to focus on your group's needs – and there's a potential for boredom.

Naturally, we want to do this right. But, before we explore exactly what constitutes the process of 'breaking the ice,' let's first agree on what this notion of 'ice' means.

Ice, in this context, refers to those intangible feelings and beliefs which people reasonably experience that limit or inhibit their interactions with others. Typically, you can expect a lot of ice to form among people who are new to each other, but it can also be present in groups who have known each other for a long time.

Little or no talking, poor eye contact, reluctance to make physical contact, lots of standing around, lack of initiative, and an absence of trust or energy are all good examples of ice manifesting itself. Ice can also look and sound like making excuses, the choice to keep to oneself, arriving late, lying, acting out and looking down at the ground to avoid responsibility.

Basically, any task that requires an individual or a group of people to step outside of their Comfort zones before they are ready to do so, will trigger a set of feelings, behaviours and survival instincts which result in an icy atmosphere. Ice is the devil of group-based programs.

Group-based programs rely heavily on interaction. If ice gets in the way of this process occurring smoothly and productively, then as program leaders we are obliged to remove as much of it as we possibly can. The more ice you break, the more fun and greater the difference you will make in your program.

What Makes an Ice-Breaker an Ice-Breaker?

So, we can agree that we need to break the ice. Well-versed in the theory that group exercises are a great way to invite people to interact, many program leaders decide to dump one or more of these experiences at the start of their program. And then wonder why people sometimes crawl back into their shells.

To truly 'break the ice' and, critically, create a platform upon which your group will thrive, an experience must reflect most, but hopefully all, of the following five criteria.

It must be:

1. **Fun** – the sort of fun I describe on page 67;

2. **Non-Threatening** – everything occurs within your group's Comfort zone;

3. **Highly Interactive** – ample opportunities for people to mix and share with others;

4. **Simple & Easy To Understand** – quick and easy explanations; and

5. **Success-Oriented** – it builds a sense of group accomplishment and worth.

In short, if an activity or experience you are considering does not tick three, four or (hopefully) all five of these attributes, don't do it. Even if you call it an ice-breaker, don't do it.

To illustrate, I need not go any further than contrast this 'ice-breaking' technology with an all-time classic ice-breaker...

First, you enter the room and survey the typical U-shaped format of tables and chairs. You choose a seat about two-thirds back from the front, not wanting to appear too eager, but not overly aloof either. A few more people arrive, and upon a few casual, quiet glances, assume their seats too. There is extraordinary interest in making oneself comfortable, aligning pens with paper and staring at the whiteboard, when finally the instructor arrives. She quickly shuffles her papers, welcomes everyone and announces her name. Then, without pausing, suggests that before she gets started, she'd like to go around the room and ask...

What do you think she asked everyone to do?

This is a no-brainer. She asks everyone to stand up, introduce themselves, and tell us where they are from and how bored they are. Grrr, I cannot tell you how angry this situation makes me feel.

I can bet, nine times out of ten, program leaders refer to this 'whip around the room introduction' exercise as their ice-breaker. But, it's not. It's simply a poor excuse for not knowing what else to do.

Now, I'm not saying that you should never present this group exercise. That is not my point. My point is, this exercise as described is NOT an ice-breaker, because it does not break the ice. Rather, it is an ice-maker!

Let's run through the checklist.

This exercise is rarely fun, except perhaps for the class clown (there's one in every group) who now views the room as a stage, upon which he or she will enjoy being in the spotlight for a moment or three.

Standing up and talking in front of others threatens people. Remember, most people list public-speaking as their number one fear, especially if they have to talk about themselves. This exercise is made even more threatening when the class clown makes everyone laugh, and now it's your turn.

This exercise is not interactive. Most people are too focused on what they are going to say – especially if they're next in line. They are not listening to anyone else. Conduct a survey of how much data is retained the next time you run this exercise, and you'll see what I mean.

To be fair, if there is one thing that this exercise can check off the list, is that the task is relatively simple and easy to understand. It may be simple to understand, but that's altogether very different to being easy to perform.

Finally, being both judge and jury in this case, I think it is safe to say that this exercise is anything but successful. Discomfort, nerves, and anything but warmth and humour will have started the day. Epic fail. Like I said, get me out of here.....

An ice-breaker is ONLY ever an ice-breaker when it truly breaks the ice. And this result can only ever be achieved when the experience invites lots of fun, simple, non-threatening and success-oriented interaction.

having fun and making a difference is not just noticed, it's experienced and felt ...

Breaking the Ice = Preparing Your Group

The sole focus, in this second step of my programming model, is to break the ice so that my group is well prepared to make the most of the program they are about to undertake (no matter the content).

As with all parts of my approach, there is a sequence involved which makes a difference. Guided by the five elements I described above, these are the four steps I commonly take to break the ice of the group I am working with.

1. Unofficial Start

Idleness will kill a program, especially if you work with young people. Attract people's attention as soon as possible, and keep them busy. Indeed, I build into all of my programs activities for people to do before the program is scheduled to start – the 'unofficial' start, so to speak.

Arrival activities, those which keep people busy while waiting for the late-comers, gently invite people into your space. There are always a number of choices, and it never matters if only some of the group actually participate. Generally, those who are busy will generate sufficient energy and buzz, and this activity will attract even more people into the space. Perfect for conferences, trainings, meetings and events.

Unofficial starts are filled with interest, choices and tons of fun. Ideally, these experiences require few props, if any, and very little supervision.

Here are some great examples of how to kick-off with an Unofficial Start:

- Set out a number of puzzles on the ground or on tables for people to engage with as they arrive.
- Smile, greet and shake the hand of every person as they walk in.
- Present a series of very short, simple and humorous activities to keep people busy as late-comers arrive.
- Distribute an activity sheet which gives people something to do after they have registered.

2. Official Start

Apart from the obligatory welcome and introduction, I like to keep people moving. You want to keep the momentum going, because if your group sits (or stands) too still for too long, you'll lose them.

Official Starts are filled with activities which focus on me (the program leader) – because this is often the safest option, particularly in a room filled with new people – and are filled with laughter and humour. If you can, pick up a few names and use them in your patter, or better still, when someone makes a notable contribution, ask them for their name, and thank them by name. Not only will you learn a new name, but so will the group.

Some ideas for Official Starts may include:

- Tell a story which frames the day's program.
- Show a short, humorous video which directs your group's attention to a particular lesson.
- Play a series of highly interactive group activities which keep people moving.
- Take a walk around your venue as you introduce the format of the day.

3. Small Interaction

By small, I particularly mean one or two people (a pair), and, on occasion, up to eight people. There's no magic in the number – it's just that if you involve too many more, the level of interaction loses some of its intimacy, and people start to feel left out. As I always say, it's hard to be left out of a pair!

These activities feature tons and tons of interaction. In a short space of time, it should be possible for every individual to have partnered, or been in a small team with, most if not all of the people in the group. Invite people to share and capture names as they move about.

There are too many Small Interaction activities to mention, but here are just a few of my favourites:

- Any activity involving two people during which they can share something about themselves.
- Pose a series of questions in which small groups gather to discuss.
- Play a series of quick, fun partner games.

4. Bigger Interaction

Now we move onto larger or (depending on numbers) whole group experiences. Your program builds on the comfort people will have developed working in groups of two or more, and can now expand to embrace a higher level of interaction with more people.

These activities still focus on tons of interaction, opportunities for people to 'volunteer' and lots of laughter.

Here are just a few Bigger Interaction favourites:

- Any circle game that involves gentle levels of activity.

- Introductory name games.

- Simple group initiatives which are very easy to achieve success in.

- Large group games which focus on healthy levels of competition.

... when you think 'ice-breaker', think of what 'experience' you could introduce that would effectively break the ice

Please note, my discussion and suggestions here do NOT mean that an ice-breaker has to be a group game or activity. For example, playing a humorous video as an arrival activity, showing a slide presentation to frame a forthcoming experience, and smiling and shaking the hand of every young person as they enter your drop-in centre, are all wonderful ways to break the ice.

So, when you think 'ice-breaker,' think of what 'experience' you could introduce that would effectively break the ice. Some of the tools at your disposal are fun group games and exercises, but you could equally introduce another form of preparation to achieve the same result.

I'm biased, but I happen to believe that ice-breakers which come in the form of group games and activities are particularly powerful at preparing a group, because they are fun to play and often engage the whole person – body, mind and soul – at the same time.

Exceeding Expectations

When presented appropriately, with full regard to the needs of your group, all of your 'ice-breaking' preparation will create a more productive atmosphere, one that is conducive to working together or whatever purpose your group has gathered to achieve.

What you want is a group of people, all switched-on and leaning-in, waiting anxiously for what's coming next. They will be prepared to entertain the notion of stepping outside their Comfort zones. Not that this is what your group is thinking. They'll be focused on their experience of feeling happy, energised and excited for more.

Either way, your group is now ready to continue on their journey with you – per chance, to listen to a keynote speaker, or work together on a project, or learn an effective problem-solving skill, or engage in a difficult conversation. All this, and much more, awaits your group in the next step (Pump).

Focus of Your Leadership

Naturally, your leadership is still focused on your group, but now, you can adopt an 'act and reflect' approach. You present something, observe, reflect. You present some more, then observe and reflect.

Your group, if appropriately prepared, will not need any assistance from you to participate because, by definition, your group is participating within their Comfort zone. All impediments to participating fully have been removed, so your group is equipped to act. In effect, you are their Coach.

As their Coach, you'll sometimes choose to 'get your hands dirty' with your group – often times just to enjoy the sheer fun of the moment. So, if your group has, for example, turned to their partners to share in a quick 'thumb-wrestle,' find a partner and share in the game too. On other occasions, it will be more appropriate for you to take a step back and observe.

Mostly, your role is about showing the way. Your example will prove very powerful to your group, not to mention, bringing you closer to the action so that you can more fully appreciate how your group is feeling at any point in time.

Like a good coach, you start with a plan, execute it and make adjustments as necessary.

Here are a few other Coach-like responsibilities:

- Think about what behaviours and interactions you need to observe within your group.

- Keep your difference (your goal) front of mind at all times.

- Determine what meaning, if any, you want the various experiences you are delivering to have.

- Consider the most logical sequence of these experiences to gradually build your group's comfort levels.

- Be prepared to re-arrange your sequence at a moment's notice, as the need arises.

Practical Prime Considerations

Before you move onto the next step (if required), consider the following pointers about this crucial preparation step:

- The 'nirvana' of this Prime step is inviting your group into the space of 'play.' You see, by definition, play is not an activity – it is a state of mind. When people enter into this space, they are wholly permeable, lacking in pretence and fully able to absorb your message. These moments of play occur when people are caught up in the flow, as described on page 47. These moments are purposeless, attractive, voluntary, free of self and time and your group will want them to last forever. Like I said, this is the nirvana of programming, and is rarely reached – but it shouldn't stop us from trying.

- For programs which gather people for only a short period of time – conferences and short events, for example – the first two steps of Plan and Prime may be all you need to apply. You may have no time or need to expand the potential of your group into their Stretch zone, so these efforts would be fruitless anyway.

- Your two most powerful tools at this stage of your program are Challenge by Choice and FUNN. Together, these two philosophies will remove many of the impediments to participation, keeping your group within their Comfort zone at all times.

- Generally speaking, it is not necessary to speak to any part of your philosophical framework. Elements such as Challenge by Choice and FUNN should be very apparent to your group, without you having to mention them by name. Implicitly, the essence of your approach will whisper to everyone that it's okay to get involved. That said, there are some groups that require your permission to have fun, so feel free to be very explicit in these cases.

- Avoid elimination games like the plague. I love these types of activities, and feature them in many of my programs, but never in the critical beginning stages of my group process. Being eliminated is one thing, but copping this over and over and, perhaps, reinforcing what ordinarily goes on for someone (outside of your program), is stepping into Panic zone territory.

- One of the most common features of ice-breaking experiences involves the learning of names. My advice – schedule dedicated name-game type activities later into your program, not earlier. The learning and remembering of names in a social context sits way outside the Comfort zone of most people. Don't get me wrong – learning names is very important, but there are many, many other ways of capturing names, which I describe in Part Four.

- Keep in mind, while infinitely malleable, resisting change (stepping into the Stretch zone) is baked into our DNA as human beings. We're open to change, but we need to adjust to the prospect slowly, if possible. To this end, go easy on your group. In my experience, while most groups are willing to embrace change, they sometimes just need a little more time and preparation to get there. The more you can respond to their question 'What's in it for me?', the sooner they will arrive. That's why giving people a choice and making it fun is so important.

- To help you make decisions regarding the actual sequence of your activities, refer to the GRABBSS model in Part Four. It's a simple and effective assessment tool that you can use to help choose experiences which are appropriate for the unique characteristics and skills of your group.

- You may be wondering how long each of the sequenced steps of the four ice-breaking stages last. This is too difficult to answer, because every group and program is different. But, I will say this – you should continue to break the ice for as long as it takes. Anything sooner, and you'll stunt the rest of your program.

PRIME: Setting the Tone Template

Difference: to help your group feel warm, switched-on, enthusiastic and happy.

1. Unofficial Start

Objective: to help people feel comfortable immediately – the moment they arrive.

- quick, simple, passive and fun
- choice of activity
- immediately attractive and engaging
- low-supervision
- low-prop or no-prop

2. Official Start

Objective: to help your group feel welcome and eager to start.

- quick introduction
- gentle, but fast-paced
- fun as major component
- focus attention on leader
- creative medium

3. Small Interaction

Objective: to help your group feel comfortable and relaxed interacting with partners and small groups.

- partner or small group activity
- fun as a major component

- opportunities for sharing
- emphasis on mixing
- success-oriented

4. Bigger Interaction

Objective: to help your group feel comfortable and relaxed interacting with bigger groups.

- large and whole of group activity
- fun as a major component
- opportunities for sharing
- emphasis on mixing
- success-oriented

Download your free copy of this Prime Template from **www.seriousfunbook.com**

Step 3 – Pump
Doing The Work

"One finds limits by pushing them."

– Herbert Simon, psychologist

You are now ready to do the work.

Work that matters, because it matters to your group.

The first two steps – Plan and Prime – will have worked their magic to have prepared your group as much as possible. It is difficult to underestimate their power to set your group up for success.

Yet, jump to this step too early (which many program leaders do,) and you can expect trouble. The sort of trouble that occurs when people are pushed outside of their Comfort zones and do not want to be there. Your efforts to appropriately and sensitively set the tone and break the ice instantly changes this landscape.

Now, chomping at the bit, this third step will uncover your group's hidden potential. It's not rocket science, but the work involved subscribes to the common understanding that the more you train and flex your muscles, the stronger you will get.

In essence, this step asks the question, what is possible?

Pump to Make a Difference

Doing the work in this step is guided by a sequence of four developmental skills:

- De-inhibitizers
- Communication
- Problem-Solving
- Responsibility

You'll find a template for this third step at the end of the chapter.

Pumping = Growth

Let's re-visit why we are here.

You have made a conscious decision to make a difference. Your group is thirsty and they are staring at a small bottle of water. However, you believe your group is sitting on a well, which no one can see. You have primed the pump and are now willing to put in the work to fulfil a promise, to tap more water than they could ever imagine.

The pumping starts now.

Remember, all activity within one's Comfort zone requires no assistance. This third step deliberately invites your group into their Stretch zones, and therefore, by definition, requires their trust and your guidance to be successful. And the more success they find in this space, the more comfortable they will become.

If you have stuck to your plan and properly prepared your group, they will be willing to trust you to dip their toes into the Stretch zone. Everything has gone well so far, they are thinking; so, they are more likely to respond positively to your invitation to stretch a little further.

From a leadership perspective, your most vigorous 'pumping' role will be to help your group create and maintain a safe, supportive and fun environment within which to function. This space, if crafted intentionally, will build trust and strengthen the relationships of your group, all of which stimulates growth, i.e., an expanding of one's Comfort zone.

In the world of difference, this growth is the very ingredient which will stratospherically catapult the level of fun and meaningful interaction your group will experience in your program. To this end, your two most valuable tools will be the Full Value Contract (FVC) and the Experiential Learning Cycle (ELC)

Appropriately prepared, your group will be in a great space to engage in a conversation to commit to, or create their own FVC. And armed with a clear and powerful behavioural framework, you can leverage the ELC to help your group draw meaning from some of the more significant, substantive moments of their experience together.

Note: The growth I point to in this step benefits nearly every group. Granted, groups which gather for longer periods of time will gain more from this process, but every group – students, staff, conference delegates, strangers, volunteers, young and old – can benefit from developing their interpersonal skills.

Continuing to adopt a sequenced approach, let's now explore the four development skills of this step.

1. De-inhibitizers

It all starts with an invitation for your group to take their first baby-steps outside of their Comfort zones. I call these experiences 'de-inhibitizers.'

While it is fair to say that the process of 'breaking the ice' removes people's inhibitions too, de-inhibitizers go one step further. They intentionally ask your group to assume greater risks – emotionally, mentally and physically. And, depending on the purpose of your group, spiritually could also be added to this list.

De-inhibitizers are the ice-breakers of the Pump step. Slowly, but surely, they keep people moving and, importantly, interacting with one another.

While still fun, these experiences should cause some people to think twice before committing. Naturally, some people are ready to move forward at any time, so these de-inhibitizing experiences are aimed at bringing up the rear, those still lagging behind in their Comfort zones.

De-inhibitizers involve small elements of risk, as well as opportunities for commitment. Back in the days of 'breaking the ice,' nothing was at stake, but feelings of discomfort or frustration may now occur. Success and failure are less important than making an effort, and within a fun environment, people are more willing to give something a go. Designed well, a co-operative and supportive atmosphere tends to encourage participation.

Here are some great examples of experiences which could be classed as de-inhibitizers:

- Making yourself look silly in front of others, e.g., contorting your body to act like an elephant.

- Approaching a stranger, introducing yourself and asking for their name.

- Exerting oneself in a wide-area tag game to avoid being tagged.

- Contributing a crazy idea which may solve a simple group initiative.

- Raising your hand to ask a difficult question.

2. Communication

With a view to intentionally building the interpersonal skills of my group, my next step is to introduce experiences which highlight effective communication.

There is nothing in this world in which we do not communicate – verbally or non-verbally – to ourselves and to others. Also, there has never been a group I have worked with that did not benefit from improving this essential skill. The more effective an individual or a group communicates, the more successful they will be.

Experiences which develop communication skills provide an opportunity for people to share their thoughts, feelings and behaviours more effectively. These activities and experiences deliberately focus on listening skills, both verbal and non-verbal, as well as key decision-making skills.

Within the context of a powerful debrief (ELC), individuals and groups can participate in their own learning, and discover new ideas which help them communicate more effectively.

safe, supportive and fun environments actively inspire people to step outside of their comfort zones ...

Some great examples of experiences which focus on the development of communication skills include:

- Practising the art and science of 'active' listening.
- Participating in an exercise / project which requires the group to reach consensus.
- Taking turns to lead the weekly sales meeting.
- Repeating back what someone just said to explore comprehension.
- Giving and receiving constructive feedback to an individual or group.

3. Problem-Solving

Seth Godin, best-selling author and inspirational thought leader, says that there are only two things our schools should teach – leadership and how to solve interesting problems. I whole-heartedly agree. With a fuller understanding of how to communicate more effectively, I now ramp up the challenge for my group and focus on their problem-solving skills.

As noted in an earlier section, these experiences should focus as much on problem-*finding* skills as problem-*solving* skills. These experiences provide an opportunity for your group to co-operate, compromise and generally solve more difficult problems.

The premise baked into this step is that problem-solving skills are wholly transferrable. What one learns in solving a problem over here may be applied successfully over there. Problem-solving experiences generally create higher levels of frustration which teach focus and patience. Adopting a trial-and-error approach to learning will also inspire creative thought, co-operation and persistence.

Here are a few examples of experiences which focus on problem-solving skills:

- Working on a project team to solve a complex problem, e.g. how to convert more enquiries into sales.

- Co-operating with several authors to write a document, e.g. a book, a mission statement, etc.

- Applying Edward de Bono's 'Six Thinking Hats' technology.

- Working with others toward an ambitious goal.

4. Responsibility

This final step in the process of strengthening your group's 'muscle' builds upon the gains developed by the previous skills.

Experiences which focus on responsibility aim to empower your group to look after itself, from both a social (group) and personal (individual) point of view. In my opinion, there is no greater paradigm for a human being than to take responsibility for oneself. This is not to say that your group is left to their own devices, but that it is capable of taking responsibility for its actions, and the consequences which flow from them.

Social and personal responsibility skills sit atop of the human developmental tree. Experiences which invite your group to work effectively with the various strengths and abilities of the individuals are a key to this step. In addition to those skills which have already been discussed, expect conversations concerning planning, empathy, support and leadership to come up a lot.

Some program leaders confuse this level of group functionality as an absence of conflict, but this is not true. There is conflict in every level of a group's development, but a group which has developed high regard for its social and personal responsibility will manage their conflict with grace.

Experiences which focus on personal and social responsibility include:

- Participating in community service projects, e.g., tree planting.

- Inviting people to call 'Group' whenever they feel the group is not functioning well.

- Trusting someone they do not know very well.

- Developing a peer-support or mentoring program between younger and older students.

Exceeding Expectations

One of the most powerful benefits of adopting this approach to group programming is the ability for groups to surprise themselves.

Safe, supportive and fun environments actively inspire people to step outside of their Comfort zones, to test their limits, to stretch beyond their self-perceived boundaries. It's not uncommon to hear groups say that they achieved so much more than they ever thought was possible.

This is how you exceed expectations. And the best part is, as their facilitator, your group will think that they did it on their own.

Do the work, pump like crazy, build your group's muscle. And during this process, I expect you'll see more fun, more participation, more value. In this order.

Focus of Your Leadership

Armed with an approach framed by the philosophies of the Full Value Contract and the Experiential Learning Cycle, your role in this step will be as Facilitator.

Accepting that any work within the Stretch zone requires assistance, your role will be to quietly guide your group to develop their skills to a level where they can reach for their biggest goals, and hopefully, make a difference.

This is not a role we read a lot about, so here are some of your more important Facilitator responsibilities:

- Consider the most appropriate experiences for your group to develop these four skills.
- Consider the most logical sequence of these experiences to gradually build your group's skills.
- Be prepared to re-arrange your sequence at a moment's notice, as the need arises.
- Never under-estimate the power of humour and fun to set the tone or break the tension.

- Ask questions which invite your group to discover the answers for themselves.

- Challenge your group to be honest with itself.

- Make observations which challenge your group's thinking.

- Develop a contingency plan if an experience does not go according to plan.

Practical Pump Considerations

Here are a few things to note in your spare time as a facilitator of growth:

- Having exercised their muscles, help your group to understand that sometimes this process will hurt a little. Growth always involves some form of pain, and this is true for group development, too.

- Expanding on the last point, this is the reason that this step in the programming model is more valuable for longer-term programs, e.g., school classrooms, corporate teams, residential groups, etc. When things get a little sticky, there is always time for the group to sort itself out, learn from the experience and move on.

- Given the dynamic nature of human beings, there is no hard-and-fast rule that says one experience or activity develops one particular skill more than another. The beauty of much of this work, especially if you utilise group games and activities, is that most experiences can be designed for a wide range of uses. For example, the activity Finger Snaps can be an ice-breaker, an energiser and a problem-solving activity. The critical ingredient will be your primary objective for introducing this experience, and your briefing of the activity as part of your overall sequence.

- Once again, to help you make decisions regarding the actual sequence of your activities, refer to the GRABBSS model in Part Four. In particular, study the discussion about the sequence of stages in which groups develop, as it applies to your group.

- As with many of the steps described in this book, you may be wondering how long you spend on developing each skill? This is still too difficult to answer. But, I will say this – you should work on developing each skill in sequence, before moving onto the next one.

That said, none of these skills are mutually exclusive, i.e., there are elements of all skills in most experiences. So, my advice is, focus on the primary benefit of a particular experience before considering where in your sequence it is best placed.

• For a simple three-step model you can use to frame your processing or debriefing activities, refer to Part Four.

PUMP: Doing the Work Template

Difference: to help people feel supported, valued and connected to other members of their group.

1. De-inhibitizers

Objective: to help your group feel comfortable about stepping outside of their Comfort zones.

- fun as a major component
- opportunities to take some risks
- focus on effort, not success / failure
- highly interactive
- some discomfort and frustration

2. Communication

Objective: to help your group feel effective in their ability to communicate thoughts, feelings and behaviours.

- verbal interaction is a major component
- introductory problems to solve
- some frustration
- opportunities to give and receive feedback

3. Problem-Solving

Objective: to help your group feel effective in their ability to solve problems and make decisions co-operatively.

- decision-making is a major component
- complex problems to solve

- opportunities for cooperation
- higher levels of frustration
- trial-and-error learning

4. Responsibility

Objective: to help your group feel comfortable enough to exercise personal and social responsibility to self and others.

- focus on taking responsibility
- opportunities for leadership
- emphasis on support and empathy
- testing of self-perceived limits

Download your free copy of this Pump Template from **www.seriousfunbook.com**

Step 4 – Peak
The Difference

"Step by step and the thing is done."

– Charles Atlas, bodybuilder

This final step in your program is the opportunity to see the difference you've been looking for.

If you have planned, primed and pumped like crazy, then your group will be seriously ready to peak. Working well together, having fun and feeling great, you and your group now have the opportunity to make an impact.

It's time to lead. Run that weekly youth meeting, teach that swim class or math lesson, hold that conference, deliver that staff training program, conduct that bush-walk or first-aid training course, and so on.

From a classroom to a corporate training room, or a conference auditorium to a weekly youth group meeting, the more effort and time you invest in creating a safe, supportive and fun environment for your group, especially early on, the more powerful and rewarding your program or event will be.

Research clearly shows that those programs which intentionally develop healthy and trusting relationships out-perform all other programs on so many levels, including greater participation, stronger communities and increased overall performance.

But, really, the most rewarding outcomes are experienced in the way your program leaves people feeling. Engaged, empowered, valued and meaningfully connected to others are all up for grabs.

Reaching the Oasis

This final phase of our programming model is akin to an oasis. It's the alluring vision of our weary desert traveller who longs to quench his thirst. Follow the plan, prime the washer and pump like crazy, and he'll create more water than he could have ever imagined.

As reflected in the story, creating an oasis from a small bottle of water involves trust, effort and risk. As such, some may argue that this phase of the journey is in fact a mirage, an illusion conjured in the mind of an unrealistic person. Fair enough, in the absence of a guaranteed alternative, I can see why some folks may form this opinion.

In my opinion, this perspective would be akin to choosing to lay down by the water pump and give up. Why would you do this? This approach is certainly easier, but it makes no difference (to the traveller). When faced with the vision of an oasis, why would you want to stop travelling towards it?

Well, it's a choice, I suppose.

No matter if you teach, train, present, lead or coach, the Difference Model offers you a choice.

Follow a plan, use the tools available to you, and do everything you can to prepare your group to give them the best chance of not only getting what they came for, but oh, so much more.

Making a difference is a choice. I hope you make it, because it matters.

... the most rewarding outcomes are experienced in the way your program leaves people feeling

Peak to Make a Difference

Unlike my three earlier steps, there are no further steps necessary to guide you in the delivery of your program.

You start with difference, and you end with making a difference. In the middle, your strongest allies are the five key programming tools.

Now, go lead. Leave your group feeling amazed, inspired and empowered.

Exceeding Expectations

This is my vision of having made a difference…

Your group will buzz with excitement. People will feel safe to contribute, make mistakes, step outside their Comfort zones, grow and discover what is possible.

Students will be doing more than just learning the three Rs, they will be developing critical interpersonal skills such as leadership and problem-solving abilities. School will be fun, and they'll look forward to returning to class every day.

Organisations will be filled with satisfied, valued and motivated people, all eager to 'lean-in' and add extra value to everything they do. For corporations, this will mean higher productivity and healthier bottom lines, while for community organisations, this will mean stronger missions and making a bigger difference to their communities.

Youth groups, clubs and organisations will attract diverse groups of young people all having a great time and looking after each other. They'll play, share, trust and learn a wide array of skills which will set them up for life. They will become highly valued and productive members of their communities.

And to think, this vision started with one irresistibly fun and highly interactive idea.

This idea has the potential to exceed your group's expectations, too. Seriously.

Focus of Your Leadership

You are now a partner with your group on their journey.

No doubt, you have a unique and special role to fill within the life of your group, but leadership or training or teaching is not your goal. It is to serve.

To paraphrase the passage at the end of this chapter, program leaders, whatever variety, lead best when they forget about themselves and focus on their group, their needs and their goals. To lead is to serve, to give, to achieve together.

Difference is listening to what your group really wants, and then creating it.

Practical Peak Considerations

A couple of thoughts to consider before we get into the more practical section of this book:

- Keep it fun, and have fun. Take fun more seriously. It's the reason I'm still in this game after so many years, and it's the reason people keep coming back.

- The Difference Model is not a 'set and forget' mechanism. You need to keep working at it, keep choosing to make a difference every minute of the day. There will be ups and downs, and there are no guarantees. It is not the answer to everything that keeps you up at night. That said, I am hard-pressed to find a situation in which this approach to programming does not have a positive impact.

- While approach is important, your content is king. Don't forget that. Adapting what George Leonard said when he was referring to competition, "Like a little salt, it adds zest to the game of life. But when the seasoning is mistaken for the substance, only sickness can follow." Do not mistake this (or any) approach for the substance of your program – it is simply a tool, a way to deliver your content. If you're a basketball coach, the reason young people turn up at your class is to learn how to play basketball. If you're running a conference, the reason delegates register for your program is to network and develop their professional skills. There are any number of reasons why people attend your programs. Over time, one of them may be that you become known for making a difference, and exceeding people's expectations. But, the essence of your program will and must always be the reason for your program. And then, the manner in which you lead it will determine how much of a difference you can make.

- Finally, you might not be able to change the way the world values your profession or role, but you can change the way you are valued by doing work that matters.

PEAK: The Difference Template

Difference: to help your group feel engaged, empowered, valued and meaningfully connected to one another.

There are many ways to create a difference, just as there are many ways to lead your group. Yet, captured so eloquently within the following passage, is the essence of a most successful template for leading a group and making a difference.

I went on a search to become a leader.

I searched high and low. I spoke with authority. People listened. But, at last, there was one who was wiser than I and they followed him.

I sought to inspire confidence but the crowd responded, "Why should we trust you?" I postured and I assumed the look of leadership with a countenance that glowed with confidence and pride. But the crowd passed by and never noticed my air of elegance.

I ran ahead of others pointing new ways to new heights. I demonstrated that I knew the route to greatness. And then I looked back and I was alone.

"What shall I do?" I queried. "I've tried hard and used all that I know." And then I listened to the voices around me. And I heard what the group was trying to accomplish. I rolled up my sleeves and joined in the work.

As we worked, I asked, "Are we all together in what we want to do, and how we'll get the job done?" And we thought together and we struggled towards our goal. I found myself encouraging the faint hearted. I sought ideas of those too shy to speak out. I taught those who knew little at all. I praised those who worked hard.

When our task was completed, one of the group members turned to me and said, "This would not have been done but for your leadership." At first I said, "I did not lead, I just worked with the rest."

And then I understood – leadership isn't a goal. I lead best when I forget about myself as a leader and focus on my group, their needs and their goals. To lead is to serve, to give, to achieve together.

– author unknown

to lead is to serve,
to give, to achieve together ...

part four
PEAK

The Oasis

"You're here to make a difference,
not just to fill in time between the meals."
– Mark Collard, trainer

The proven way to add value is to do work that matters.

Work that matters is difficult to do.

My intention here is to help you.

This final Part of the book applies the tools and the four step sequence of the Difference Model to many familiar problems, situations and what if? scenarios.

First, I return to the seven mistakes program leaders make and consider some alternatives. Then, I explore dozens of practical solutions to answer many of your most frequently-asked questions – everything from Where do I start? to What do I do now?

I share the best of my knowledge drawn from 25+ years of trial and error programming with tens of thousands of people from all over the world. I expect that you will discover many terrific ideas which speak to you and your issues. Some ideas will challenge you, while others will confirm that you're on the right track.

Lots of 'how-to' ideas and many valuable hints, strategies and leadership tips. Short, sharp and sweet.

8

Seven Differences Program Leaders Make

"There are no traffic jams along the extra mile."
– Roger Staubach, NFL quarterback

In Part Two, I explored seven common mistakes program leaders make as experienced in some all-too-familiar situations. With each situation, I discussed the impact of a poor programming approach as it applied to the powerful Zone of Proximal Development (ZPD) theory.

Now, with the tools and the four steps of my programming model under your belt, let's re-visit these situations, turn back the clock perhaps and offer some solutions.

1. Not Breaking the Ice

Situation: one minute into his training session, an instructor asks everyone in the room to stand up and introduce themselves.

Alternatives:

• Invite people to participate in a series of simple table-top activities as they arrive. This keeps the group busy, generates much-wanted energy, and provides an opportunity for the trainer, not to mention the group, to meet and greet people informally.

- Formal names and introductions (if necessary) can be left until later in the morning when people have warmed-up.

- Invite people to introduce themselves in paired and small group exercises.

- In absence of these alternatives, invite only a couple of volunteers to introduce themselves (as in original situation) to get a feel for the group. No pressure for everyone to respond.

2. Lack of Philosophical Framework

Situation: a class of dysfunctional students attend a three-day camp to participate in a variety of team-building initiatives.

Alternatives:

- Present a series of very fun, highly-interactive, hard-to-stand-away-from activities in the first session. This will grab the students' attention quickly, not giving them too much time to think.

- Next, establish a Full Value Contract with the students to set clear goals and behavioural boundaries. Students will set agreed-upon consequences when expectations fall short.

- Present a series of challenging activities over the course of the weekend which provide an opportunity for the students to frequently reflect on what is and isn't working, and what lessons can be applied to their own lives.

3. Unrealistic Expectations

Situation: a half-day conference is scheduled urgently to develop short and long term action plans for an organisation.

Alternatives:

- Upon invitation, the facilitator should only commit to outcomes that can be realistically achieved in three hours. Otherwise, the facilitator should decline the gig because they are unlikely to exceed expectations.

- Recommend delaying the meeting for a few days or lengthening it to accommodate more time for preparation and planning.

- Only invite people who can realistically influence the decision-making process or outcomes. This will hasten the decision-making process and avoid wasting the time of too many people.
- Ensure that adequate time is provided for every person to have their say i.e., if they are invited to attend, they must also be invited to contribute.

4. Poor Needs Analysis

Situation: two days before school starts, a group of teachers are required to attend a workshop to study horse-whispering.

Alternatives:

- Survey the teachers to understand what professional development courses, if any, they would really value doing.
- Thoroughly investigate the efficacy and methodology of any professional development options. Partake only in those which make a difference to what the teachers care about. This ensures buy-in from the teachers.
- Allow each teacher to attend by choice, and ensure that they are given options to determine their own level of participation during the course. This may need to be communicated to the service provider.
- Consider an alternative time in the school year to conduct the professional development, i.e., to avoid over-burdening the teachers at a critical time of their year.

5. Not Valuing People's Time

Situation: the convenor of an annual conference waits until everyone is present before starting the program.

Alternatives:

- Prior to the scheduled start, present a series of 'unofficial start' activities to keep people occupied, e.g., give 'permission' to everyone to meet and network with others sitting close-by, or present a very simple, fun activity which people can do in their seats. This will build relationships and generate lots of energy.

- Start on time. This is what people expect, and values everyone's time, including the first keynote speaker.
- Later, acknowledge late-comers, and suggest that they catch-up with a colleague who could fill them in on what they missed.

6. Neglecting the Power of Story

Situation: a local pastor is invited to share her understanding of a parable to her local youth group.

Alternatives:

- Weave a compelling story into the presentation to help the young people connect the lesson to their lives.
- Even better if the story relates to something or someone they know.
- On occasions, ask the youth to form small groups to discuss one or more questions posed by the pastor. Small groups are a safer option for people to share, and test ideas.

7. Absence of Fun

Situation: on the first day of the school year, a PE teacher runs a series of games to mix a small number of new students in with her established class.

Alternatives:

- Ensure that all of the activities are focused on inclusion, and engage the students in lots of fun, highly-interactive activities. Move quickly between activities, to give the students little time to think about what's happening.
- Pause on regular occasions in randomly created small groups, and invite the students to share their responses to one or more questions posed by the PE teacher. The more sharing, the better.
- Avoid any form of elimination games, at least in the first week of classes.

work that matters is difficult to do.
turn the page for some tips & strategies ...

9

How Do I Do This?

*"The only place where success comes
before work is in the dictionary."*

– Vince Lombardi, NFL coach

Whether you're a new or experienced program leader, there are always
lots of questions.

Two of the most important questions I have already answered are, "How
do I break the ice?" and "How do I design a remarkably fun program?"

Here are twenty-one more questions I want to tackle:

How do I...

- Get started?
- Set goals with my group?
- Use the right activity at the right time?
- Create a Full Value Contract?
- Conduct an effective debrief?
- Make debriefs interesting and fun?
- Get everyone to participate?
- Keep my group focused?
- Adapt activities to suit my group?

- Know when to stop an activity?
- Divide large groups into smaller groups?
- Form random partners?
- Break up cliques?
- Manage people who arrive late?
- Manage large groups?
- Remember names?
- Manage people who are forced to attend my program?
- Manage people who don't get along?
- Manage difficult behaviours?
- Achieve too much in too little time?
- Find the right activity?

The pages which follow provide one or more answers to each of these questions, in the order that they are listed.

If your question is not listed here, or perhaps the solution doesn't work for you, then I hope you will contact me and ask for help. Write to me at **hello@playmeo.com**.

How Do I Get Started?

No matter how much experience you have, knowing where to start is often the most difficult part. Here are a few tips to move you forward:

- Do something immediately. The first chance you get, even if you don't fully understand all of the steps, do something which reflects a learning for you in this book. Present a new ice-breaker, add arrival activities to your next training session, start on time, weave a story into your lesson, etc.

- Start with the 'thing' you feel most comfortable with. The longer you wait, the more difficult it will be for you to develop a new skill, or break an old habit.

- Do something fun. Take your class outside for a walk, play a group game, re-arrange the furniture in your training room, ask a colleague to co-lead with you, etc.

- Even if things don't go smoothly, look for signs that your group was having fun. Focus on that.

- Before your next program, consider more deeply what your group values and really cares about. What's it like to be them? What matters to them? If you're an experienced practitioner, compare these observations with your existing program goals – how do they stack up?

- Practice, practice, practice. Accept any opportunity to expand your experience and repertoire.

- If you're just starting out, volunteer at first, and start building your experience, not to mention, your networks.

- Be yourself. Sure, in the beginning, you'll try to imitate those you look up to, and this is natural. In time, you'll develop your own style which, soon enough, others will look up to.

- No one else has the same background, experience, values, personality, enthusiasm and drive as you do. Make the most of it.

Still not sure? Visit **www.playmeo.com/program-templates** to download forty of my favourite program templates (as described on page 195), each one of them jam-packed with tons of fun and value.

How Do I Set Goals With My Group?

The most effective goals are those which are SMART and easily identify the difference they will make to your group, i.e., how they will leave your group feeling. We also know that to achieve buy-in, it's a good idea to involve your group in the goal-setting process.

Here are five of my favourite methods or techniques for setting goals with my groups:

Personal Action Plan

I ask each person to write down and / or respond to the following four questions:

- What do you want to accomplish during this program, and why does this matter to you?
- How will you accomplish your goal, and what actions are you willing to take?
- What resources and support from others will help you achieve your goal?
- How will you know if you have reached your goal, i.e., what will it look, feel and sound like?

Palm Tree

I ask each person to place their hand palm-down on a single large sheet of paper and trace around the perimeter of their hand with a marker. Encourage every hand-print to touch at least one other hand-print (to build metaphor of inter-connectedness). I then ask each person to write one goal (or feeling that matters to them) inside their hand-print and sign their name. After sharing these goals with one another, we post the sheet in a prominent place to keep the goals in existence.

The Being

One person lies down, face-up, on a large sheet of paper (or several pieces taped together). Carefully, the rest of the group traces around the perimeter of this person. The person gets up. I instruct each person to write one goal along the traced edge of 'the being.' Then we write as many attributes of healthy relationships on the inside of the being, and on the outside all of those things which get in the way of healthy relationships. After a thorough discussion of the merits of what has been written, we post 'the being' in a prominent location.

Partner Introductions

In pairs, I ask my group to spend five minutes getting to know their partners. Normally, they can share anything they wish, but I typically ask that they extract three specific bits of information – their name, a favourite movie and a professional goal they would like to achieve during the program. Upon returning to the large group, I ask each person to introduce their partner (not themselves) to the rest of the group.

Moonball

Each person writes one effective team-oriented attribute on a beach-ball. We discuss the value of each attribute, and then commit to upholding them. Then, I present an initiative – for the group to keep the ball off the ground for as long as possible, by hitting it with an open-hand. Scoring a point for each hit, the group is challenged to reach a target, or score the highest possible score. Making several attempts, the score returns to zero each time the ball lands on the ground. To conclude, my debrief connects the attributes written on the ball with the way the group worked together to achieve their goal, i.e., did they 'uphold' their values or not?

How Do I Use
The Right Activity
At The Right Time?

Adopting a sequenced approach to your programs requires an ability to assess and read your group at any given time. In the interests of selecting the right activity at the right time, I can think of no better instrument than GRABBSS.

Created by Project Adventure, GRABBSS is a self-assessment tool that you can use to make informed decisions about the 'right' thing to do in any given moment, and when to make adjustments to your program.

GRABBSS is a series of questions divided across seven key elements you can observe and evaluate about your group. One element is not necessarily more important than another, but the acronym reads as follows:

Goals

What is the purpose of this activity? How does this experience relate to the goals of the group? Will it make a difference to the group?

Readiness

Is the group ready (mentally, emotionally, physically) to undertake the experience? What needs to change before the group has the ability to undertake the next stage of the program?

Affect

What is the feeling of the group? What sensations are they experiencing – boredom, excitement, apathy, resistance, etc? How do these feelings impact what they do next?

Behaviour

How are the group or individuals acting? Are the interactions among members positive or negative for the group? How co-operative are they? Will their behaviour be appropriate for their next experience?

Body

What are the physical abilities of the group? What physical characteristics of the group will impact the program? Are the individuals tired, do they look after their bodies, do any individuals have a disability, are they hot or cold, etc?

Stage

What stage of development is the group experiencing? It is useful to refer to Bruce Tuckman's popular rhyming schema to describe the varying levels:

- Forming – beginning of a group's existence, most activity fits within Comfort zone;

- Storming – often involves conflict as the group enters their Stretch zone, and individuals start to assert their opinions and leadership;

- Norming – group cohesion is forming, as group identifies more productive ways to function;

- Performing – group is functioning effectively and efficiently; and

- Transforming – the point at which the group ceases to exist.

Does the group need additional skills to function at a higher level (stage) of development? Generally speaking, the higher the level of group development, the more challenging your experience can be.

Setting

What is the physical setting of the program, and the 'cultural' background of the participants? Are you inside or outside, secluded or likely to be disturbed? Is the space limited? How long have the people known / worked with each other?

In essence, you are constantly asking yourself these types of questions to help you make an informed decision about what is appropriate or 'right' for your group as you proceed.

For example, you may be working with a school group for the purposes of developing problem-solving skills. Even though the agenda says that you should do a particular activity straight after the break, if the group has not demonstrated that it has the skills necessary to succeed, i.e., the group is not ready, then you are well advised to alter your program sequence. Slot in some extra activities to better prepare your group, or present an alternative exercise in place of the less-appropriate one.

Or, perhaps the group is ready to move onto the next experience, but has 'cooled' down significantly during your debrief. Then, throw in a quick 'warm-up' to move their bodies once again before proceeding.

How Do I Create A
Full Value Contract?

The creation of the Full Value Contract tends to fall into one of two categories:

Pre-Determined

This form of Full Value Contract does most of the work for your group in advance. While quick and efficient, you will want to invite your group to discuss what each of the tenets means to establish some form of 'buy-in.'

Here are four examples:

- Play Fair, Play Hard, Play Safe

  – ideal for very short programs involving very young people

- Respect for Self, Others & the Environment

  – ideal for short programs involving young people

- Be Here, Be Safe, Be Honest, Set Goals, Care for Self & Others, Let Go & Move On

  – ideal for young people and adults

- Be Present, Pay Attention, Speak Your Truth, Be Open to Outcomes, Create a Safe Environment

  – ideal for adults involved in longer programs

Group-Generated

This category reflects the essence of the Full Value Contract, whereby an agreed framework is created entirely, or in part, by your group. This process establishes a higher degree of buy-in, but it will take more time. Ideal for longer-term programs, or in situations where buy-in is essential to your group's success.

Here are some examples:

- Adapted
  - you may wish to start with a pre-determined framework (above), and invite your group to modify or build upon it, coming up with their own words.
- Do It Yourself
  - starting from scratch, your group forms the words to their own behavioural framework. Ideally, these norms are written down, but oral agreements work too.
- Experiential or Activity-based
  - activities such as The Being and The Palm Tree (see page 144) form the basis of your group's discussion to capture a set of agreed-upon norms. Presented visually, this technique can be very engaging because it involves multiple styles of learning.

How Do I Conduct An Effective Debrief?

Just as the activities in your program need to be sequenced carefully to be effective, you should also approach your debriefing as a sequence.

Here's a three-step method which follows a simple, easy-to-remember sequence:

1. **What?** – reflect on the details of 'what happened' in the experience(s).

2. **So What?** – generalise these facts, make connections and look for patterns.

3. **Now What?** – apply this information to the next activity, or ultimately, to people's real lives – at school, home, work and play.

Ease into your debrief by beginning with the facts. Ask 'What?' type questions to start with. This will get people talking, and, to be honest, this is often the hardest part. Some examples may include, "What did the group do when the second beach-ball was introduced?," "What methods were used by the group to solve the problem?" and "How did the group come to a decision?"

Then, if appropriate, you can move the discussion onto the next step – generalising or adding meaning to what happened. The 'So What?' step pre-supposes that we do something with what we hear, to interpret the facts, look for patterns and perhaps make it mean something.

"When groups are in discussion, it is best for one person to speak at a time" is a good example of an effective meaning at work.

At this point, it is important to ask questions that help your group find its own answers. This is a good place in which to address issues such as trust, communication, safety, leadership and co-operation. These 'So What?' type of questions may sound like "What made the method of solving this problem so effective?" or "Why did the group become frustrated?" or "How did it feel to be left out of the decision-making process?"

The most powerful step is moving your group on to consider the 'Now What?' stage. A standard question to ask is "What have we learned in this activity that we can apply to...?" Sometimes, these connections are very clear, while other times your group may have no idea. Again, this is where you come in.

Use questions that help your group to see the big picture, such as, "Give me an example of how we could improve our co-operation based on what we just discussed" or "What will we do differently as a group next time?" and "What goals can we set to improve your overall performance?"

Do not expect to see the blinding light every time you sit down with a group to discuss what's happened. But, if you are keen to draw more than just a fun time out of your program, invite your group into their Stretch zone a little by adding a structured debrief from time to time. It will not only give you tons of valuable information about how your group is travelling, but will expand your group's Comfort zone too.

Note, even with a powerful structure, your debriefs may not necessarily be fun. This is the focus of the next question.

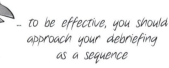

... to be effective, you should approach your debriefing as a sequence

How Do I Make Debriefs Interesting & Fun?

Conducting a debrief with some groups (especially young people) can often feel like pulling teeth or herding cats – they either don't want to co-operate, and / or they will scatter all over the place.

Your debriefs need a good structure, reflecting a few key elements to keep your group engaged. While there are no hard and fast rules, the following tips and advice are useful to consider:

Stop Talking at People and Start Talking *with* People

Invite people into your conversation, rather than just telling them what they need to know. For example, compare "This is how you hold a surfboard." with "Jesse, what do you think is the best way to hold a surfboard?"

Ask Lots of Open-Ended Questions

The question "How are you feeling?" is more powerful than "Are you feeling cold?" Open-ended questions are more likely to provide greater insight and opportunities for people to participate in an interesting two-way conversation.

Use a Variety of Formats to Keep it Fun

Debriefing is more than just asking your group to circle up and respond to a few questions. The first step in learning is engaging the brain, so choose a variety of discussion techniques that are fun, interactive and meaningful to attract your group's attention. Here are some fun debrief activity ideas featured on playmeo:

- Whip Around – around the circle, one at a time, ask each person to make a response.

- Coloured-Ball Debriefing – people pull out a random item and discuss a topic according to its colour.

- Hula-Hoop Debrief – feedback is offered as a hula hoop is passed through the hands of your group.

- Fill The Gap – one at a time, ask each person to add their response to the start of a sentence.

- One Minute Debrief – fast-paced strategy to extract a lot of ideas in a short time.

Make it Easy to See and Hear Each Other

Consider using circles to conduct your conversation, and moving in closer to hear each other. Also, be aware of the impact the wind and the sun may have on your group's ability to see and hear you. For example, it is recommended that you face into the sun, rather than your group, otherwise it will give them just another excuse to look elsewhere. And keep their backs to the distraction of other people, interesting panoramas and other events that will easily distract them from your conversation.

How Do I Get Everyone To Participate?

In my experience, this question reflects possibly one of the biggest issues program leaders face every day – how do you engage unmotivated or unwilling people to participate in your program?

Starting from the premise that these people can participate, they are just choosing not to, I prefer to point the finger of blame at my program or my approach first.

Here are a few of my favourite strategies to get these 'un' people involved:

- Make your program as outrageously fun, and non-threatening, as possible. As discussed on page 67, fun is very difficult to stand away from, and it's often very difficult to look cool when everyone else is having a fun time. This strategy works nine times out of ten, and is by far the simplest, and most enjoyable technique.

- Connected to the strategy above, honour Challenge by Choice – allow people to join your program out of choice, rather than forcing their participation. Many people hear Challenge by Choice as 'I don't have to do it' which is true, but then I take it as a personal mission to make my program so irresistibly fun, it will be hard to sit on the sidelines. Initially, some people prefer to 'sit it out,' but slowly, as they discover that my program is actually a lot of fun and isn't going to threaten them, they change their minds and get sucked into the program. Indeed, I can think of only two or three occasions in my career when I was not able to help people make an appropriate decision.

- Check in with the unmotivated, and, where appropriate, explain to them that Challenge by Choice is as much a Challenge *of* Choice. Help them to understand that there are many levels of participation they can choose.

- When appropriate, challenge people's choices. This is a particularly powerful strategy for young people, who are just starting to learn that they will be held accountable for their decisions. The reply 'I don't want to do it' doesn't cut the mustard, I need to know why. Pushing this line of questioning is a judgment call, but some people, when they realise they are just being stubborn, will change their minds.

- Involve your group. Sometimes, without even asking, other members of the group will urge the less willing to join in, or at least learn a little more about what's going on for them. The fact that this encouragement is coming from their peers is as powerful as their (leading by) example.

- One on one, ask the unwilling or unmotivated to respond to this question – On a scale of 0 to 10, with 0 being the minimum and 10 being the maximum, where would you rate your level of enthusiasm for the program? If they are being honest with themselves, you can expect answers somewhere in the range of 2 to 5. Now, you may assume my next question is to ask, why didn't you choose a higher number? But no, a more powerful question to ask is, Why didn't you choose a lower number? You see, this question directs the individual to acknowledge that they do actually have a small degree of enthusiasm for the program (otherwise, they would have selected a lower number). Ah, ha – gotcha! It's from this point that you can build a conversation around what would be necessary to have them choose a number high enough to get them involved.

How Do I Keep My Group Focused?

Focus can be affected by many factors. Presuming you have done everything to remove all external factors – such as other attractions, standing in front of a beautiful background, overlooking basic needs such as food, water and shelter – then focus is mostly related to the 'What's in it for me? question.

Here are my favourite strategies for maintaining the focus of my group:

Keep it Fun

If you're feeling good and enjoying something, then you are very likely to want it to continue. Fun, in the way it is described and delivered in this book, has a knack of doing this for people. In my world, too much fun is never enough. It's only when the 'fun' factor starts to fade, that people start to question the relevance, benefit or meaning of an experience.

Connect the Dots

When people start to question why they are doing something, they will struggle to maintain interest. Even when you're having fun, it is still necessary for you to connect this experience to your overall program goals, even if it's only to jump up and down for ten seconds to generate energy for the next session.

Furthermore, frequently throughout my program I find it useful to connect what we have just done, or what we are about to do, with the overall purpose of the program.

An even more powerful approach is to ask the group why they think we did or are about to do something.

Preserve the Adventure

While connecting the dots, maintain as much mystery and adventure in your approach as possible. Half of the fun of a truly successful program is found in the rudiments of surprise and discovery of what you do, and don't do. Everything from inviting a volunteer from the crowd before you have described what they are going to do, through to keeping the punch line (so to speak) of your activity right to the end. This approach will keep your group focused and build excitement for what's coming up next.

Build Trust

By far the most powerful strategy I know for keeping a group focused is earning the trust of my group. This comes under the heading of the old adage – a group doesn't care what you know until they know how much you care, i.e., once again pointing to the 'What's in it for me? question. There is no doubt that I am able to maintain my group's interest for longer periods of time the more I invest in the development of a fun, safe and supportive environment for the group to interact within. When trust has been built, it is so much easier to introduce more challenging tasks such as 'focus on this for a long time.'

Take Breaks

This can be achieved as easily as stopping on a frequent basis to literally take a break, or changing the pace of what you are doing. It is strongly believed that we should not expect people to maintain continued focus on any one topic or activity for much longer than 15 minutes. For this purpose, you might note that all TED Talks are mandatorily less than 20 minutes. Also, simply moving from one fast-paced activity to a slower one and then back again can refresh the focus of your group.

Be Gentle

As adults, we can have pretty high expectations of young people sometimes. Accept that young people, generally speaking, are still developing their focus and concentration skills. As program leaders, we have a responsibility to teach these skills, bit by bit, and not in one big experience.

How Do I Adapt Activities To Suit My Group?

In stark contrast to the 'one-size-fits-all' approach to programming, I believe (a) it is necessary to adapt your program to the unique needs and abilities of every group, and (b) there are many ways to avoid the dreaded 'I've-done-this-before' syndrome.

Adapting Your Program

Take a look at the GRABBSS model as discussed on page 145. This check list will help you to 'read' what's happening in your group, and how you may need to alter your planned sequence of activities.

Beware of the 'cut-and-paste' or 'auto-pilot' short-cut to program design. Let's be honest, many programs start from a basic framework, but as soon as you begin to cut stuff from one program and paste it into another, you may get some very odd results.

For example, drawing from personal experience, a corporate group being referred to as 'children' throughout parts of my written proposal/quote, or the choice to roll out a particularly awesome legs-in-the-air kind of exercise (because it's worked in the past) before realising that most of the women in my group were wearing skirts. Oops!

Adapting Your Activities

There are a number of variables you can use to tweak the challenge or the framing of an activity:

- **Time** – introduce a time limit to reflect stress and real world deadlines, or remove one to assess how well the group copes with open time lines.

- **Resources / Equipment / Space** – supply more or fewer resources, including information, equipment, technology and even physical space limitations.

- **Handicaps** – denying the use of speech, vision or the use of a limb for one or more people in your group (where safe to do so) will increase the challenge of an experience.

- **Obstacles** – introduce pre-determined, or random obstacles which aim to impede the progress of the group, such as water, bridges, and 'safe' and 'unsafe' contact areas.

- **Scenario** – in the briefing of every activity you have at least three framing options (a) as it is, e.g., get your group from here to there in 30 minutes..., (b) as a fantasy, e.g., you have to save the pink Zulu elephants from a tribe of rampaging pygmies..., or (c) as a metaphor to reflect one or more elements of your group's real world experience, e.g., rolling a marble down a series of plastic tubes to represent the fragile and fragmented communication systems of your group.

How Do I Know When To Stop An Activity?

My motto, always leave them wanting more.

Stopping an activity just as it reaches its peak, and perhaps a tad further, will give you many useful programmatic starting points.

Moving on at this juncture keeps the energy of your group up and their spirits high. It's easier to slide into the next exercise if you have their attention, even if they are complaining that you stopped too soon. Better this, than having no complaints because everyone left the scene on account of gradual boredom!

You can always go back to an experience if it really is that good (and it fits your program goals), but it's often better to move onto something new while you have them in the palm of your hand.

Clearly this is a judgement call. You really need to connect with what people are feeling and thinking before you can decide when enough is enough. This is the perfect time to consider the GRABBSS check list (see page 145) to identify those signals coming from your group which suggest one way or the other.

For example, when some people start to tire, or shift uncomfortably in their seats, or divert their attention elsewhere – these are all signs that it may be time to move on.

In contrast, all heads down, or a certain buzz of activity or that unmistakable sense of people engaged in a moment of 'flow' are all signs that your group is happy to continue.

And remember, quoting the evangelical words of Karl Rohnke, "if at the end of the day you have waned more often than you waxed, it's time to get a new job."

How Do I Divide Large Groups Into Smaller Groups?

We can all recall the uneven, socially destructive results when two 'captains' were nominated to pick their teams. Or, the equally predictable count-off method of "1, 2, 3, 4, 1, 2, 3..." around the circle. They rarely produced balanced teams, nor were they fun or interesting.

The best method to divide larger groups into smaller groups is to adopt a random split, for example, to ask each person to find all others who match some criteria you announce. For example, if the category is "The colour of your eyes," everyone who has blue eyes will gather together, all the brown eyes will get together, etc.

Here are some simple two-group splits:

- Arm that ends up crossed over the top of the other, when folded on your chest.
- Shower / bath in the morning or end of the day.
- Preference for cooking or cleaning up.
- Prefer a dog or a cat as a pet.
- Last digit of your home telephone number – odds and evens.
- Number of street you live at – odds and evens.
- Preference for tea or coffee.
- Preference for bad news followed by good news, or vice-versa.
- Side of bed you get out of in the morning.

Here are some simple multi-group splits:

- Month in which you were born (12).
- Season of the year in which you were born (4).
- Type of blood group.
- Oldest, youngest, or in-between in your family (3).
- Colour of your eyes, hair, hat, shirt, pants, etc.
- Which shoulder(s) you hold a carry-bag – right, left or both (3).
- Mode of transport to get to the program (car, bus, bike, walk).

And two more which are a couple of my favourites, but require a little more explanation:

- Randomly distribute a deck of playing cards to your group. Ask everyone to find someone holding a card of a similar suit, or the same face value (e.g., King, 9, Ace, etc).

- Starting with pairs (see page 167), ask each partnership to join with another. And these four people join with another four people, etc, until you have the required number of teams.

Inevitably, the two or more teams you form will be uneven. If this is a problem, use the old scientific method to even them up by saying, "Hey, you and you, can you go over there..."

... the best method to divide larger groups into smaller groups is to adopt a random split

How Do I Form Random Partners?

One of the most frightening things my PE teacher ever asked me to do was "Pick a partner." While these were the words my teacher used, what I actually heard him say was "... find someone who likes you, or is like you, or you want to hit on or ..." whatever other awkward social issue comes up for you.

As the smallest, least co-ordinated kid in class, this was always a disaster, because I was often one of the last people to be paired off. Not a real self-esteem building exercise I can tell you.

Now, I'm not saying that you shouldn't use this technique to form pairs. What I am saying in the context of this book and wanting to make a difference, is that there are many, many other ways of achieving the same result (creating a pair) which come with far more positive side-effects.

Any one of the random criteria listed in the previous section can be adapted for use to create groups of two people as well. So as to not repeat myself, here are some more ideas:

Ask each person in your group to find one other person who has the same:

- Length of hair.
- Height, or size of hands, feet, thumb, ears, etc.
- Type of mobile (cell) phone.
- Favourite car, animal, ice-cream flavour, TV show, etc.

- Choice of holiday destination selected from three possibilities, e.g., Hawaii, Swiss alps, Hong Kong.

- Favourite genre of movie, sport, book, etc.

- Number of letters, syllables or vowels in their name.

And one more which requires a little more explanation:

- With hands behind their backs, ask everyone to extend a certain number of fingers on one (or two) hands. When ready, ask everyone to reveal their variously extended digits in front of them so that others can see them – the task is to find one other person with the same number of extended fingers.

How Do I Break Up Cliques?

Cliques are those exclusive groups of people which form as part of a larger group, but do not like to mix with others. They are generally referred to by terms such as the 'cool kids,' the 'in group,' the 'upstairs department,' or even as basic as 'us and them.'

These groupings occur quite naturally in the beginning because, speaking from our Comfort zones, we all prefer to assimilate (belong) with people we like or are like.

However, if left unattended for too long, cliques can become a real wedge in your efforts to create a fun, safe and supportive environment for everyone.

Cliques are just a manifestation of 'ice,' which of course must be broken. Here are some of my favourite strategies to dilute them:

- As they say, prevention is the best cure. Introduce as many fun, highly-interactive experiences early on in your program to provide lots of opportunities for your group to mix and get to know one another. Within a fun and non-threatening environment, you can never do too much mixing.

- When you present activities which require partners or small group work, always use a random group-splitting method to prevent members of cliques sticking together by default. Refer to the previous two questions to give you lots of fun ideas to achieve this result.

- Let's say you tried the above two techniques, and many members of a clique are still clinging together. Presuming it is beneficial to split these folk up, try one of these strategies:

  - Use a 'category' to split your group into smaller groups according to some characteristic the clique can not deny, e.g., eye colour, type of shoes they are wearing, etc. For example, on a large student orientation program, I noticed three boys spending a lot of time together over the course of several mixing activities. If this behaviour continued, I believed it would really stunt the potential of my program. So, at a critical juncture, I asked everyone to find a group according to the colour of their tops. As each of the boys was wearing a different-coloured top, they were suddenly separated, and presented with their first opportunity to mix with some new people.

  - Ask everyone to stand next to a friend or someone they know to form a pair. Ask one person to kneel down, then, only after everyone is kneeling, ask the other person to move to a separate area, and voila! You have split your clique in half and formed two random teams.

  - Form a straight line according to some criteria, the more interesting, the better, e.g., date of birth, house number, etc. From here, ask people standing closest together in the line to form partners, small groups, teams, etc.

How Do I Manage People Who Arrive Late?

The principle behind my most powerful strategy to combat late-comers is to give my group a reason to be on time. Notice, this switches the responsibility onto me – a turn of events you may not be comfortable with, but hear me out.

Of course, I'm not about to blame myself for every person who turns up late, but in the world of making a difference, there are many benefits to having my whole group present when I start on time.

Here are some classic examples of how I do this, drawn from a variety of real groups I have worked with:

School Classroom

To start the day, a teacher conducts a really fun group activity which sets the tone for the day's lesson. Every student arrives early outside the door, because they never want to miss out on the fun. Otherwise, they know and will feel that they have missed something that everyone else will be talking about.

University Class

As first year university students are prone to do, they arrive late because they can. And sadly, most lecturers wait for late-comers, so why bother rushing anyway?

In this class, ten percent of the course assessment is allocated to 'participation' which is basically turning up (which quite frankly, I do not understand. What? You get points just for turning up?) Without ever asking the students to turn up on time, three to four weeks into the semester, there was rarely a student late to class because the first 20 minutes was always dedicated to playing a series of really fun activities. Like the example above, every student was motivated to arrive on time because they didn't want to miss out.

Summer Camp

There was never any incentive to turn up on time for meals at summer camp, because the kids knew that they would never be denied food. But, the dining room ran on such a tight schedule, if one group of boys was late, it would cause the next sitting of meals to be late, and so on. As discipline wasn't working, a novel idea was tried. A large whiteboard was hung inside the dining hall doors. Each meal, a puzzle or question was posted which invited each cabin group to submit an answer. The first correct answer won points which counted towards a nominal prize at the end of the session. However, the puzzle was removed 5 minutes into lunch. If you were late, not only would you miss the puzzle, but your cabin was disqualified from entering the competition. The puzzles were an instant success. The whiteboard is still used today.

Annual Conference

As a rule, a full complement of conference delegates is rarely achieved after any break, let alone the start. The typical two-minute warning music was used to encourage people to return to the auditorium, but this was never enough. So, a new strategy was tried. As people filed back into the auditorium after every break, they were given two playing cards (from a regular deck), and as soon as it was time to start, the doors were closed / locked. Late-comers were literally locked out for two minutes. During this time, the delegates inside the auditorium were invited to mix and swap cards, one for one, with others. Their goal – to end up with the best hand of Poker at the end of the conference. Naturally, if you were late back from a break, you missed out on getting two new cards, or worse, the opportunity to trade your cards with others. Worked like a charm.

Surfing Lessons

A surfing organisation conducts lessons for kids in dozens of centres across the nation. Many kids would turn up early for their lessons, but the instructors never knew what to do with them until everyone arrived. They couldn't go into the water just yet, but when they asked the 'early-birds' to come back in ten minutes, they didn't always return (because invariably the kids found an interesting rock pool, or some other distraction). Then, they hit on the idea of introducing the 'unofficial start' – one or more activities the instructors could set up on the beach in advance of the lesson to keep the early kids busy, but with minimal supervision. What they also discovered was that most of the kids started to arrive on time, because they hated to miss out on the 'unofficial' fun at the start of the lesson. Bonus!

Note, there is no magic in any of these ideas. The key is – identifying what people really care about, their point of difference, and then integrating that into the program design. Win-win.

How Do I Manage Large Groups?

The following tips capture what I believe to be the most useful, practical advice for working effectively with large groups. As adapted from my book *Count Me In*, these tips apply equally to any size group.

Just Start Playing

Don't fluff about, get your group busy as soon as possible. This advice is just as germane for small groups, but the speed at which a negative thought spreads with a large group is 10 times faster. Don't give it a chance to germinate, and your group will be swept along with a more powerful form of contagion – your enthusiasm.

Use Pairs

Paired activities – those which require two people to play – are my go-to choice when it comes to working with large groups. As mentioned earlier, it's hard to be left out of a pair, and with many pairs all doing the same thing, it creates a lot of energy. Swapping partners on a regular basis provides many opportunities for folks to interact and get to know others. And finally, if you discover an uneven number of people in your group – guess what? – it's your turn to play.

Get Their Attention

If you can't be heard or generally have to fight to get the attention of your group, then you'll find it difficult to work with groups no matter what their size. If this sounds like you, then try some of these attention-getters. Some are more appropriate for young people than adults, but all are equally effective.

- Address your group in a volume range of approximately 5 to 7 out of 10. Not only will this strategy preserve your voice, but once your group gets the idea that you're speaking, they will quieten down or shuffle in toward you. Consider talking nonsense until most of the group has your attention, lest something important is missed.

- Raise your hand, and instruct everyone to raise their hand when they see other raised hands. Like my old summer camp leader used to say, "When the hand goes up, the mouth goes shut."

- Say "If you can hear me, clap once" to invite all those within earshot to follow suit (clap). Then continue with, "If you can hear me, clap three times" (clap, clap, clap). And so on, until the room gets the message. Change the number of claps to gauge the level of listeningness.

- Count down with a loud, "FIIIIVE, FOOOUR, THREEE...." If you have them trained well, by the time you get to three, most of the group will be with you.

- Play a short piece of music, and train your group to understand that when the music stops or fades out, you want everyone's attention. Works much better than a whistle.

Position Yourself Strategically

Much of the success achieved by an 'expert' (regardless of their field) can be explained by subtlety. In the realm of programming, here are three key subtleties to take serious note of when it comes to strategically positioning yourself in relation to your group:

- Circles are good. Generally speaking, standing as part of a circle, your group has the best chance of not only seeing you, but everyone else in the group. This will lead to engagement and interest. However, once a group numbers 70 or more, it may become more difficult to hear you.

- Always look toward the sun, a bright / back-lit background or the most interesting part of the room. This strategy drives the focus of your group's attention toward you, and not these other distractions.
- Tell a secret. I love lowering my voice and inviting my group to 'bunch on in' around me. The closer my group gets, the more energy and intimacy they will generate, the less I have to project my voice, and most importantly, the more excitement I can build into my patter.

Factor in More of Everything

Large groups consume more of everything. Plan accordingly. The activities will take more time than you expect – allow at least an extra 20% than you would for 'smaller' groups. You will need more equipment to share around, especially if there is a risk of breakage or spillage – so, have more on hand than you think is necessary. And, you will need more people or leaders to help you to be heard, control the crowd, distribute and gather things, etc.

Break it Up

Owing to issues of attention-deficit, distractions, and the possibility that maybe not everyone can hear you, break everything you need to say into little chunks. Tell them only what they need to know when they need to know it. And apply the well-known saying – a picture is worth a thousand words. Provide lots of practical demonstrations of what to do and what it looks like.

Use Innovative Group-Splitting Exercises

Commit to using a variety of innovative and fun methods to separate your large group into smaller groups. Refer to pages 165 to 168 for lots of ideas. These exercises generate energy, and often lots of laughter in the process. In some cases, the group does not even recognise that they are being divided until it's too late – perfect for interrupting those hard-to-crack cliques.

Be Adaptable

In my experience, the mantra 'stuff happens' multiplies in proportion to the number of people involved.

So, let go of the idea that everything will run perfectly. It won't. The 'program' will always require your constant attention to changes that occur within the group (and not necessarily for the worse). And that's OK, provided you don't stress over it. Simply adjust your program on the run, keeping your group's goals in mind at all times.

How Do I
Remember Names?

People often remark that I have a great memory for names. I don't, I just use a couple of key techniques to help me recall them. Here are a few ideas that may work for you too:

- If possible, review the list of names of your participants before you meet them. This task will simply familiarise you with some of the names in your group, especially the more unusual ones, rather than serve as a memory test.

- For smaller groups, make an effort to greet each person as they arrive, introducing yourself and asking for their name.

- During the course of your program, especially in the beginning, frequently ask for the name of a person who makes a contribution, and then repeat it when you thank them for it. Not only will this reinforce the person's name, but it will also assist you (and the group) to pronounce the name correctly if it happens to be less common.

- If appropriate, introduce some formal or dedicated name-game exercises, but not too early. Working with names too formally too early can scare people off, and they are not necessary anyway. Most experiences can occur without the knowledge of someone's name.

- Use the names of people as often as you can, and expect to get it wrong sometimes. In fact, you want this to happen, for two reasons. First, I ask to be corrected, and learn the person's name.

Second, I then speak to the group and suggest that this interaction says that I care enough to want to know someone's name, and not that I am stupid and forgot it. In effect, this communicates to my group that (a) it's okay to make mistakes, (b) we all forget names, and (c) it's okay to ask someone whom you have already met for their name again.

- On occasions, attaching a mental image of some interaction or experience associated with a person helps me recall their name. It may take a moment to bring this image back, but it often forms a powerful hook for my memory. For example, I'll always remember Jack, a teenager I met at camp many years ago because the first time we met, he was wearing a bright red cap – so every time I look at a photograph of him, I am reminded of this initial connection, and somehow his name comes back to me. Bizarre, but true.

- Listen to your group interacting, and pick up a couple of names in their conversation. There have been many occasions when I have surprised people by using their name, and they are left wondering how I could possibly know it. "Ahhh, I've heard about you…"

A quick story to finish with. On a very large residential summer camp, many of the kids thought I had the most amazing memory because I always seemed to know their names. This was one of my sneaky strategies. I would approach a camper, and say "Hey, is that your t-shirt?" and take a quick look at the name printed on the label inside their collar. "Ah, yeah, it's yours Daniel. How's it going?…"

… use the names of people as often as you can

How Do I Manage People Who Are Forced To Attend My Program?

This is a curly one. I sit between the realm of preventing these circumstances in the first place and the reality of acknowledging that people are coerced to participate all the time.

Let's look at both situations.

What Can You Do to Prevent This from Occurring?

Without repeating myself too much, return to Part Three and re-visit the discussion about my most valuable programming tools, especially Goal-Setting and Challenge by Choice.

Ideally, every person who attends your programs will have (a) the choice to attend or not, and if they do attend, (b) the choice to determine the level of their participation. My approach to achieve this second step should be obvious. There are two actions I can take to achieve the first step (which I do not often control):

1. Communicate the rationale behind my program approach. In my initial conversations with a group, I will always describe the approach I will take to design and deliver their program, emphasising the critical benefits of difference, fun, choice and fully-valued participation. This conversation aims to influence the language used by the group when speaking about my program with their members.

If people can expect to have fun and know that they will not be threatened or forced to do anything that they don't want to do, this is normally enough for most people to willingly turn-up.

2. Even when this rationale makes sense, if the group informs me that not many people would choose to attend if they were given a choice, then I want to know why. I need to know what matters to this group, and what they really care about. If we can drill down on these needs, we may be able to uncover a powerful 'difference' for the group which will help them bridge the gap between being stuck in their Panic zones and turning-up.

What Can You Do When People are Forced to Attend?

Okay, so now you're stuck with a group of folks, all sitting there with their arms crossed on their chests and looking gruff. Other than a warm smile, you have just one powerful tool at your disposal – fun.

Of course, an atmosphere imbued with choice will help, but if you can make your program so irresistibly fun that it will be difficult to stand away from, then you will have done everything you can to make a difference. People may still choose to stand out, but hopefully in time, they will choose to join the rest of the group.

Naturally, people choosing to opt out and sit quietly in the corner is very different to those who are actively engaged in wanting to sabotage your program as an act of defiance. Again, I use fun and choice as my primary weapons to disarm this sort of behaviour, but if it gets too difficult, I will challenge a person's choice to participate in my program and remove them if necessary (but this is extremely rare).

How Do I Manage People Who Don't Get Along?

As with the last scenario, I am caught in the middle between prevention and remediation.

First up, issues of not getting along tend to occur more often with groups that experience a long time frame together, such as school classrooms, corporate and community organisations, summer camps, etc. New groups, on the other hand, or people who only spend a short time together rarely enter into the space of not getting along because they tend to interact within their Comfort zones.

In the world of prevention, my primary strategy would easily fill the pages of another book. In short, my advice is to intentionally develop community. Your most powerful strategy to manage people or groups who don't get along is to build trust and strengthen relationships, the sooner the better.

There is no special formula for creating community, but I do know that it begins with an environment that values each person, is fun and creates a safe place for people to disagree and support one another.

The tools we have discussed in this book will equip you with the ability to create such an environment. As conflict and a lack of co-operation typically occur within people's Stretch zones, your most useful tools will be establishing a Full Value Contract and invoking the Experiential Learning Cycle to process some of your group's more significant experiences.

These tools are properly described in Part Three, but let's look briefly at how they can assist you in many 'not-getting-along' types of situations right now:

- Establishing a Full Value Contract with your group will serve two important objectives. One, it will create a clear, conscious and shared agreement which will help your group identify what are acceptable behaviours, and what it really cares about. This conversation can occur at any time, but naturally, the sooner the better. Two, it will provide both you and your group with a mechanism to manage behaviours which do not meet your group's expectations. For example, if a particular member of your group is not co-operating, you can re-visit the agreement to discuss what's going on. Or, if someone is actively disrupting the group's progress, these behaviours can be compared with the checklist of acceptable behaviours.

- Simply pointing at the Full Value Contract will not, on its own, cause change. On occasions, you will want to process or debrief your group's more challenging experiences using the Experiential Learning Cycle. Actively guiding your group to reflect and debrief certain experiences will help to facilitate an exchange of ideas and the development of shared knowledge. The more lively the interaction, the more opportunity for growth. In this way, a group can explore why certain types of behaviours are not beneficial or productive to achieving group or individual goals. For example, it's not enough to say that 'put-downs' are bad and should not occur. Your process must also explore why they are unacceptable and describe their projected, short- and long-term impact on people and groups.

Clearly, these two programming skills are highly specialised and take time to develop. While I encourage you to seek further training (refer page 194), here are a couple of final thoughts:

- Your role is critical, because most people (certainly, young people) do not come equipped with an ability to reflect and process on their own, and need guidance and encouragement to navigate this path successfully. Otherwise, dysfunction may follow.

- Trust and relationships take time to develop. Go easy on yourself and on your group. Trust the process described in this book. It works, but progress is not always linear. Prepare to adjust and involve other people and tools in this journey.

How Do I Manage Difficult Behaviours?

Goodness, this topic could easily fill the pages of another book. But let's focus on just three of the more common types of 'difficult' behaviours, as adjudged by the number of times people ask me about them.

Dominant Personalities

These people talk louder, longer or more forcefully to be heard. They suck the oxygen out of the group, and they annoy everyone, including you, perhaps. Even if this person's intentions are good, letting their behaviour continue will be harmful not only to your program, but to the group. Here's what I do in these situations:

- In a group discussion, I set the stage by announcing that I want everyone to share. Indeed, I may even limit the amount of sharing each person is permitted. If the dominant person runs over their time, I catch their eye and ask them to pause, and immediately look to the next person willing to share and ask them (or the group) what they think.

- If the dominant person interrupts someone else, I will politely hold up my hand and say assertively, "Sorry, but Jane was speaking, let her speak…" and then invite Jane to continue.

- If standing, I will direct or face my body towards the person who is speaking. In this way, the dominant person will not get my attention. If they happen to interrupt, I apply the strategies described above without looking at the person.

- On occasions, these steps will help the dominant person to recognise their disruptive behaviours, and they may curb them. Generally, however, you may need further reinforcements:

  - Adopt very structured forms of conversation such as whipping around the circle, or using a 'talking stick' to indicate that only one person may speak at a time, in turn.

  - Adopt small group discussions before reporting back to the larger group. In this way, the dominant person will not impact the whole group.

  - I may deem it necessary to chat privately with the dominant person. I will affirm the value that they are adding to the conversation, but emphasise my need to involve more people. A useful strategy may be to invite their help to encourage others to share, or on one occasion, I asked that they wait for five other people to contribute before they spoke again.

  - If you have developed a Full Value Contract with this group, consider asking this person to reflect on their behaviours in the context of the 'respect' and 'equal opportunity' (or similar tenets) which form part of the agreement. Ask for their help in keeping the agreement.

Quiet / Reserved / Shy People

Sometimes, these more introverted folk behave in this manner because their contributions are squeezed out, and they have just learned to remain silent. It is important that everyone feels valued in a group, so here are some tricks of the trade to elicit their involvement:

- Invoke lots of partner discussions. Pose a question or topic and ask each person to pair up with one other person to discuss their response.

- If I suspect the quiet person (in a pair) will probably speak last, or hope that the time runs out before they have to, I choose an attribute that this person has which will invite them (and all others who apply) to share first, e.g., the partner with the longest hair, or wearing the lightest coloured top, etc.

- Adopt a whip-around strategy to structure the time each person may share. If they share very little, or I feel that there is more to say, I may ask them to elaborate a little more.

- In private, I may ask one or two of the more confident people in the group to look out for the quieter types, and actively seek out their contribution in group conversations. This help, when it comes from their peers, can often be more powerful than when it comes from you, the program leader.

- If this reserved behaviour is becoming dysfunctional either for the individual or the group, then I may choose to chat privately with them to explore what's going on for this person. It may be that they are naturally quiet and reserved, but it may also be an outward signal that something is troubling them.

the Full Value Contract will be a powerful tool to help you develop healthy behaviours and positive interactions ...

Bullies

A bully is someone who intentionally picks on or causes emotional, verbal or physical intimidation or harm to another.
The purpose of this section is not to replace the existence of an effective anti-bullying policy. However, it is fair to say that as bullying occurs in many settings – in school, at work and at play – these behaviours may raise their ugly heads in your group-based programs.

First of all, any form of bullying behaviour must be immediately stopped, and never tolerated. Their incidence should be reported to whatever authority has been established for this purpose in your setting.

Secondly, creating a fun, safe and supportive environment – as discussed in this book – will not only build trust and strengthen relationships within your group, but will significantly diminish the opportunities for bullying to flourish.

A strong framework such as the Full Value Contract will be a powerful tool to help guide you to develop healthy behaviours and positive interactions among members of your group. The Full Value Contract is particularly powerful because it empowers your group to not only create its form, but to manage its operation. In effect, it is created by your group, for your group.

The incidence of bullying is unlikely to be shared within the context of the group, so it is further hoped that as a responsible member of your group, a victim of bullying will feel comfortable to approach you as the program leader, if these behaviours occur.

How Do I Achieve Too Much In Too Little Time?

In a world that expects more from less every day, it's not surprising that our programs are under pressure too.

My first response to this dilemma is to always set clear boundaries at the beginning of your program which reflect your realistic expectations of what can be achieved, i.e., fewer hours means fewer outcomes. My advice also extends to never committing to an outcome you can't exceed. This is not the same as 'under-promise-over-deliver' – it's about making a difference.

You see, making a difference means being really clear about how you will leave your group feeling at the end of your program. Your group will expect you to achieve their goals, and you will. But, you will also leave them feeling valued, inspired and empowered, which they may not be expecting.

You may find that by embracing the 'difference' technology described in this book, you will actually achieve a lot more than you ordinarily would. When you create a fun, safe and supportive environment, and you take the time to build trust and strengthen relationships, you will be able to leverage your group's hidden potential to get a lot more done.

For example – many teachers tell me that they are sceptical in the beginning, because in a 50 minute class, they could not imagine giving up 5-10 minutes "to have fun" and still get everything done.

But, trusting the process and pumping like crazy, many of them quickly discover that this investment of time and effort pays off big-time because it often makes the remaining 40 minutes of their class more productive.

Or, more often, they discover that the time they spend early on having fun, building trust and strengthening relationships pays bigger dividends later into their semester because they spend a lot less time managing difficult behaviours in their class.

Similar benefits have been reported within corporate environments. The more time and effort an organisation spends to leave their staff feeling valued and empowered, the more powerful the results – higher staff morale, higher productivity and higher staff retention. All of which adds up to better salaries (to keep good staff) and healthier bottom lines.

These are just two examples of exceeding expectations, and achieving a lot in a limited space of time.

Too much in too little time? It's all a matter of perspective.

I mean, how is it that Sir Richard Branson can achieve so much more than you and I, when all three of us have exactly the same number of hours in the day? The number of hours in the day is never going to change, so that just leaves our approach to those hours, right?

... never commit to an outcome you can't exceed

How Do I Find
The Right Activity?

You can never have enough fun group activities up your sleeve to help you use the right activity at the right time in your program.

playmeo hosts the largest online database of group-based activities in the world.

You'll find hundreds of...

- Outrageously fun and highly interactive ice-breakers and get-to-know-you games;
- Quick and easy minute-movers, warm-ups and energisers;
- Powerful trust-building and community-building games; and
- Innovative and engaging team-based problem-solving activities & puzzles.

You get step-by-step instructions for all of the activities, plus video tutorials, leadership tips, sample lesson plans and debriefing tips.

The database is totally searchable to help you find the right activity to meet your group's needs. Refine your search by type of activity, number of people, time and equipment needs. Drill down even further by adding important key words.

From a two minute energiser at the start of a class, to a week-long residential team-building program, you will find dozens of ideas to motivate your group to have fun, interact and make a difference.

The activities are universally appealing, require few if any props, and suit people of all ages.

Go to **www.playmeo.com** for more information.

10

Where To From Here?

"Your present circumstances don't determine where you can go;
they merely determine where you start."

– Nido Qubein, speaker

First of all, thank you for taking the time to read *Serious Fun*.

I hope that you have enjoyed the journey, and have been inspired by what I have shared to help you squeeze the most value out of your new and existing programs.

We are all different, and every group is unique. There are many ways to lead groups, so what works for one may not work for another. Nevertheless, I have worked hard to share only those nuggets of wisdom which I honestly believe to be the most powerful strategies for achieving programmatic success.

Now, it's your turn. I invite you to embrace the Difference Model. Naturally, adapt it to your group's unique needs, characteristics and aspirations, and make it your own.

And be sure to share your successes with those around you. Indeed, write to me at **hello@playmeo.com** when you discover a new idea or something that really works for you, and I'll share it (with your permission) with tens of thousands of other program leaders connected to the playmeo network.

Remember, a good idea doesn't care who it belongs to, so pass this book onto one of your colleagues when you're done. Recalling our Desert Pete allegory, this is akin to re-filling the water bottle before you move on, to leave something for the next weary traveller to quench their thirst.

Recommended Next Steps

When you are ready to take the next step, go to www.playmeo.com and enrol in one of the following one-on-one and / or group-based professional development programs:

Online Tutorials

A series of short, self-paced online tutorials designed for program leaders who don't know where to start, or have just begun leading groups and need some practical advice. These innovative sessions can be accessed 24/7 on any internet-enabled device, and may be repeated as often as you wish. Ideal for beginners, but equally valuable for experienced practitioners.

Training Workshops

Face-to-face, practical training workshops lead by Mark Collard or one of his international team of expert facilitators. Options range from one-day introductory open-enrolment programs to advanced multi-day workshops which can be custom-designed for your particular training needs. All custom workshops come bundled with a package of exclusive content including online resources, activity books and one-on-one professional development coaching.

One-on-One Coaching

A series of regular live coaching calls with one of our international team of experts. These calls are designed to reinforce the content of a practical training workshop you experienced, or to help you manage a range of opportunities or issues in your new or existing programs. You can book a single session, or lock into one of our popular three, six or twelve month plans.

Go to **www.playmeo.com** to learn more.

11

Bonus Program Templates

"Price is what you pay.
Value is what you get."

– Warren Buffett, investor

Often the hardest part of designing and leading a program is knowing where to start. While there are clear risks in becoming too prescriptive, there is value in sharing a series of program templates which have worked for me, and – perhaps with a little tweaking – will work for you, too.

Here are forty of my best. All of these programs, and many more, are available at **www.playmeo.com/program-templates**

Get-To-Know-You Programs

Highly-interactive sessions which invite a group of strangers to get to know one another. Emphasis on non-threatening fun, mixing and sharing.

10 minutes, 12 people	30 minutes, 12 people	60 minutes, 12 people
10 minutes, 30 people	30 minutes, 30 people	60 minutes, 30 people
10 minutes, 100+ people	30 minutes, 100+ people	60 minutes, 100+ people

Fun Community-Building Programs

Fun, highly interactive group-based sessions which strengthen relationships and generate lots of positive energy. Ideal for weekly and evening programs for established groups.

20 minutes, 12 people	30 minutes, 12 people	60 minutes, 12 people
20 minutes, 30 people	30 minutes, 30 people	60 minutes, 30 people
20 minutes, 100+ people	30 minutes, 100+ people	60 minutes, 100+ people

Team-Development Programs

Interactive sessions which purposefully develop trust, communication and problem-solving skills.

20 minutes, 12 people	30 minutes, 12 people	60 minutes, 12 people
20 minutes, 30 people	30 minutes, 30 people	60 minutes, 30 people
20 minutes, 100+ people	30 minutes, 100+ people	60 minutes, 100+ people

Conference Energisers

Simple, fun exercises ideally suited to large groups of people in restricted / seated environments.

1 minute, 100+ people	2 minute, 100+ people
5 minute, 100+ people	10 minute, 100+ people

Warm-Up & High-Energy Programs

Full-on, high-energy sessions which aim to raise a sweat and a lot of smiles.

5 minutes, 12 people	10 minutes, 12 people	20 minutes, 12 people
5 minutes, 30 people	10 minutes, 30 people	20 minutes, 30 people
5 minutes, 100+ people	10 minutes, 100+ people	20 minutes, 100+ people

12

More Resources

Also by Mark Collard

No Props: Great Games with No Equipment (2005)
Count Me In: Large Group Activities That Work (2008)

To order, go to **www.playmeo.com/group-games-books**

playmeo.com

playmeo.com is an innovative online platform that equips program leaders with the skills and strategies they need to deliver remarkably fun and meaningful group-based programs.

You will find a variety of practical resources, including:

- Free downloads, webinars and podcasts;
- Access to the largest online activity database in the world;
- Online tutorials for beginners and experienced practitioners;
- Practical training and professional development workshops; and
- One-on-one 'fast-track' coaching programs.

To browse, download, subscribe and enrol, go to **www.playmeo.com**

Publications

My book shelf is groaning under the strain of dozens of publications related to group programming and activities.

There are just too many to mention here, but it would be fair to say that many of the best have been published by Project Adventure Inc, including:

- *Silver Bullets 2,* by Karl Rohnke
- *The Hundredth Monkey,* by Nate Folan & friends
- *Adventure in the Classroom,* by Mary Henton
- *Exploring Islands of Healing,* by Jim Schoel & Richard Maizell
- *Gold Nuggets,* by Jim Schoel & Mike Stratton

Go to Project Adventure Inc www.pa.org for more details.

Inspiration

Seth Godin, author of fourteen international best-sellers including *Linchpin* and *The Icarus Deception.* Subscribe to his blog at www.sethgodin.com and click on his head.

Bernadette Jiwa, best-selling author of *difference.* You can find Bernadette and her award-winning blog at www.thestoryoftelling.com

Dr Stuart Brown, founder, National Institute for Play and author of *play* www.nifp.org

Zone of Proximal Development, first developed by psychologist Lev Vygotsky (1896-1934) www.wikipedia.org/wiki/zone_of_proximal_development

David Kolb, originator of the Experiential Learning Model www.wikipedia.org/wiki/experiential_learning

Daniel Priestley, entrepreneur and best-selling author of *Become A Key Person of Influence* www.keypersonofinfluence.com

Gratitude

Gratitude is one of the most powerful emotions one can bring into their life and offer to others. I acknowledge my deepest gratitude to the following people, most of whom I have even met.

First and foremost, to **Gilly** and **Devon** – for loving me, being there always and allowing me the space to get stuff done when I needed to. You two, especially, I can never thank enough.

To **Alan** and **Joy** – for being my parents, and raising me the way you did. You need to know that you 'did good,' and there is no doubt that I am who I am because of who you are. Together with Gill and Devon, I can't imagine my life without you.

To **Seth Godin** – for not wasting a word, and making a difference. Your thought leadership has helped me to get out of my own way, and understand that not adding value is the same as taking it away.

To **Karl Rohnke** – for throwing a stone into the pond of adventure programming so many years ago. You could never have known how far that initial ripple would travel. I have thoroughly enjoyed surfing it.

To **Bernadette Jiwa** – for so eloquently spelling out the difference creating a difference makes. You helped me discover the story I wanted to tell to create my own *Difference Model*.

To the **Key Person of Influence** team – for creating a simple, yet powerful framework to help me tell my story, attract opportunities and do what I love.

To **Rufus Collinson** – for editing and finessing my words, all the time aligning them closer to the English lexicon.

To **Peter O'Connor** – for capturing the essence of my message in one simple, fun book cover, and for elevating the prominence of a rubber chicken to front-cover status.

To **Michelle Pirovich** – for wrestling with my words, paragraphs and chapters, not to mention an unruly bunch of illustrated rubber chickens, and aligning them in such a simple, yet stunning format.

To **Nick Street** – for creating the aforementioned rubber chickens, and a number of key diagrams, all of which reflect the not-too-serious tone of the book.

To **Barbara de Vries** – for allowing me to use your beautiful, distraction-free study to pen this manuscript.

And finally, to the many thousands of people I have had the privilege to work and play with over the years – for allowing me the opportunity to hone my skills and slowly unpack my leadership process into a four-step sequence that scales.

Thank you.

... thank you

About The Author

Mark Collard is one of the most experienced and qualified adventure educators and training consultants in the world. He is an expert at helping program leaders design and deliver remarkably fun programs that make a difference in the lives and performance of their groups.

Mark is the author of two top-selling activity publications – *No Props: Great Games with No Equipment* and *Count Me In: Large Group Activities That Work* – published by Project Adventure Inc.

In 2012, he founded playmeo.com, an innovative online platform that equips program leaders around the world with access to a variety of online resources, practical training workshops and one-on-one professional development coaching programs.

Mark brings a natural warmth and energy into everything he delivers. His fun and vibrant approach not only makes people feel at home, but also assists them to learn more from their experience.

A highly sought-after trainer on the national and international circuit, Mark is also a fun and super-passionate keynote speaker, voice-over professional and Master of Ceremonies.

On a personal note, Mark has been struck by lightning twice, he has found five four-leafed clovers (so far), and estimates that he has spent more than five months of his life (so far) sitting inside a steel tube hurtling through the air at 800 kph as he has criss-crossed the globe on his travels.

Mark lives with his beautiful wife and son in Melbourne's outer east, and counts his time travelling and delivering programs with groups all over the world as some of the most rewarding and funnest times of his life.

Contact Details

Mark would love to hear from you if you have any questions, or would like to learn more about his online resources, training workshops and one-on-one coaching programs.

- PO Box 4237, Croydon Hills VIC 3136 Australia
- +61 413 075 123
- hello@playmeo.com
- @playmeo
- www.facebook.com/playmeo
- www.playmeo.com
  www.seriousfunbook.com
  www.markcollard.com

Notes & Doodles

need a great starter's

Notes & Doodles

Notes & Doodles